Dealing
With
Destructive
Cults

Dealing With Destructive Cults

Una McManus
John C. Cooper

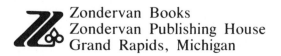

Zondervan Books
Zondervan Publishing House
Grand Rapids, Michigan

Zondervan Books are published by
Zondervan Publishing House
1415 Lake Drive, S.E.
Grand Rapids, Michigan 49506

Dealing With Destructive Cults
Copyright © 1984 by The Zondervan Corporation

Library of Congress Cataloging in Publication Data
McManus, Una.
 Dealing with destructive cults.
 Bibliography: p.
 1. Cults—Controversial literature. I. Cooper, John Charles. II. Title.
BL85.M4   1984   291   84-3552
ISBN 0-310-70281-X

Edited by Anne Severance and Evelyn Bence

Printed in the United States of America

84 85 86 87 88 89 90 / 10 9 8 7 6 5 4 3 2 1

To my parents,
Martin and Myra McManus
        —Una

and

To my mother,
Mrs. Marguerite Anna Gerard Cooper,
and in memory of my father,
Mr. C.M. Cooper (1901-1982)
        —John

Contents

Preface

My telephone rings. It's a worried mother. Her daughter is involved with the Children of God. What should she do?

I explain her alternatives, while stressing the seriousness of the situation. But she will not, or cannot, acknowledge that her daughter is in danger. From her tone of voice, I can tell she will do nothing.

A few months later, her fifteen-year-old daughter flees to another city with the cult. By then the girl is pregnant and lives with a leadership couple as the man's second "wife."

This book could have helped. It tells how to cope with cults—from a first encounter to the readjustment problems following a cultic experience. From the questions following my lectures and the mail generated by my autobiographical book describing my years in a cult, *Not For a Million Dollars,* I saw a need for a comprehensive book that would help and inform families of cult members, ex-members, religious and helping professionals, concerned Christians, and citizens. Drawing on my own experiences as a follower and as a middle-level cult leader, the experiences of other ex-members, and the research of psychiatrists, psychologists, sociologists, clergy, lawyers, and scholars of the cults, I have set out to answer the questions most asked. This is the book I wish I—or my parents—had read, the book I wish had been available for the mother of the fifteen-year-old girl.

Una McManus

Acknowledgments

The authors express gratitude to the following organizations and publishers for the use of quotations from copyrighted sources:

Christianity Today for quotes from "Countering the Cultic Curse" by Grant R. Osborne, © 1979 by *Christianity Today,* used by permission; The Bobbs-Merrill Co., Inc., for quotes from *Beloved Son: A Story of the Jesus Cults* by Steve Allen; the American Civil Liberties Union for quotes from *Deprogramming: Documenting the Issue*; Beacon Press for quotes from *Strange Gods: The Great American Cult Scare* by David G. Bromley and Anson D. Shupe; American Family Foundation, Center on Destructive Cultism for quotes from *Destructive Cult Conversion: Theory, Research, and Treatment* by John G. Clark, Jr., M.D.; *NY University Review of Law and Social Change* for quotes from "Colloquium—Alternative Religions: Government Control and the First Amendment;" *Science Digest* for quotes from "Information Disease: Have the Cults Created a New Mental Illness?" by Flo Conway and Jim Siegelman; J. B. Lippincott Co. for quotes from *Snapping: America's Epidemic of Sudden Personality Change* by Flo Conway and Jim Siegelman; Prentice-Hall for quotes from *Religious and Spiritual Groups in America* by Robert S. Ellwood; Federal Bureau of Investigation for quotes from *Law Enforcement Bulletin*; Dorset for quotes from *Moonwebs: Journey into the Mind of a Cult* by Josh Freed; *Fordham Law Review* for quotes from "Deprogramming Members of Religious Sects;" Regal Books for quotes from *Lord of the Second Advent* by Steve Kemperman; W. W. Norton and Co., Inc. for quotes from *Thought Reform and the Psychology of Totalism* by Robert J.

Lifton; Impact Books for quotes from *Not for a Million Dollars* by Una McManus and John Charles Cooper; Transaction Books for quotes from *In Gods We Trust: New Patterns of Religious Pluralism in America* edited by Thomas Robbins and Dick Anthony; Fortress Press for quotes from *Prison or Paradise? The New Religious Cults* by James A. and Marcia R. Rudin; SAGE Publications for quotes from *The New Vigilantes: Deprogrammers, Anticultists, and the New Religions* by Anson D. Shupe, Jr. and David G. Bromley; Chilton Book Co. for quotes from *All God's Children: The Cult Experience* by Carroll Stoner and Jo Anne Parke; Cooper Square for quotes from *American Culture and Religion* by William W. Sweet; Macmillan for quotes from *Scientific Study of Religion* by Milton J. Yinger.

Gratitude is also expressed to participants in personal interviews with the authors and to Max Parks, psychologist, Akron, Ohio.

If truth be mighty and God all-powerful,
His children need not fear that disaster will
follow freedom of thought.

—*François de Salignac de La Mothe Fénelon*

1. First Encounter

The daughter of an oil tycoon forsakes her wealth for a life of vagrancy with the Children of God.

A brilliant chemical engineering student abandons his education to sit in a mindless stupor before the photograph of a rotund guru.

A devoted nurse gives up her profession and now lives only to wash, dress, and offer food to the statues in a Krishna temple.

A young married man leaves his wife and children, denouncing them as evil, and spends up to fifteen hours a day selling flowers and candy for Rev. Sun Myung Moon.

Nine hundred people—men, women, and children—desert their native country to follow a maniacal messiah into the jungles of Guyana and, following his interpretation of "the will of God," commit suicide.

As an idealistic teenager, I left the security of home and family to chase a dream that became a nightmare in the Children of God/Family of Love.

Why do such bad things happen to people who desire only to do good?

Those listed above and many others who have become involved with destructive cults are quite ordinary, mentally sound people who craved a better life for themselves. Most of the people attracted to and recruited by cults have their primary needs for rest, food, and shelter met. But their psychological needs of self-esteem, ego enhancement, and sense of purpose are unfulfilled. Unfortunately they were approached by a cult recruiter at this time of great spiritual hunger. The recruiters were more than adept at spotting starving souls and moved in to exploit them.

Getting involved in a cult is largely a case of being in the wrong place at the wrong time.

BAITED AND HOOKED

A recent study by the University Religious Council at the University of California, Berkeley, found that people who follow cults have often been recently hurt or disoriented by a personal crisis. According to the study, under the right circumstances almost anyone is subject to the approach of a cult recruiter.

Those "right circumstances" abound in the lives of young people—the uncertainty of the last year in high school, the turmoil of adolescence, the loneliness of the first year at college, the devastation of a broken romance or marriage. Any one of these events can render an individual temporarily susceptible to the lure of the cults.

In exchange for unhappiness and confusion, cult recruiters offer these young people: unconditional acceptance; group identification; easy, absolute answers; friendship; affection.

A popular misconception regarding cult members is that they are troubled individuals, borderline psychotics, or emotional cripples. The average cult member is not characterized by debilitating problems or low intelligence. Many are merely misguided idealists.

After studying the cult phenomenon, Dr. John Clark, associate clinical professor of psychiatry at Massachusetts General Hospital—Harvard Medical School, claims that the "vast majority of the people in the cults are assembled from adequate families and have not shown any sign of pathology in their growth. As a matter of fact, they have often been some of the very best of our growing generation, the most imaginative, the most likely to use their minds, and they have enjoyed good relationships with their families."

"There is no one type of person who gets involved with cults," adds Dr. Margaret Singer, clinical psychologist and professor at the University of California's medical school in San Francisco and in the psychology department at the University of California, Berkeley. Dr. Singer, who has worked with hundreds of ex-members, suggests, "Almost anyone in a period of loneliness is in a vulnerable period in which he or she might get taken in by the flattery and deceptive lures that cults use . . . I've found that the people who've gotten involved with cults have tended to be somewhat depressed . . . (and) in between a major anchoring point and affiliation."

SERVICE OR SELF-INTEREST?

As a rule, modern destructive cults do not want the emotionally infirm, the dull-witted, the poverty-stricken, or the drug addicts, contrary to their altruistic claims. Cults are not service organizations, and their leaders are primarily interested in swelling their ranks and increasing their revenues, not in providing services for the needy. Upon inspection, the service programs of which they boast are frequently fictitious or mere tokenisms.

While I was a member of the Children of God, we raised money by asking the public for donations to "help with our work with drug addicts." The truth was that, while some members had been involved with drug use, everyone was required to abandon such habits upon joining the group, and no concentrated effort was made to help drug addicts. David Berg himself, our leader, communicated this information to the veterans of the group. In fact, during my initial months of training, I was instructed explicitly by my immediate superior not to "waste time" on drug addicts, since they were too hard to train.

The monetary and expansional interests of the cult leaders require that the followers be of reasonably sound mind and body in order to recruit the greatest numbers of new members and bring in the largest sums of money.

NEW MEMBER OR VICTIM?

The question remains: Why would anyone in his or her right mind join a cult and submit to such manipulation and exploitation?

The answer lies partly in the fact that people rarely *join* cults. For the most part people are *trapped* into these groups. "Joining" something requires making a decision, a choice. It necessitates receiving enough information to make that decision. Many cults routinely withhold or misrepresent information about themselves and their activities from potential recruits until the conversion is largely completed.

A blatant example is the West Coast branch of the Unification church which has hidden its affiliation from potential recruits and donors. Although this deception has been documented by the media, the leaders make no apparent effort to enforce upon their solicitors higher ethical standards. Mose Durst, West Coast Unification leader in the 1970s, denies this charge.

Some cults do not reveal the name of their leader or the purposes and practices of their group until the convert is firmly enmeshed. Most of them do not inform a potential convert of the consequences of "membership."

This deception through omission is in direct opposition to the practices of many main-line denominations. A person desiring to become a Roman Catholic or a Lutheran is required to attend a series of classes which give a thorough understanding of the church and its theology. A convert knows the full nature of his or her commitment before becoming a member. This type of advance information and depth of instruction is not afforded most cult recruits.

Carla W., an ex-member of the Children of God/Family of Love cult, said that had the cult's shrouded activities been revealed to her at the beginning of her involvement, she would never have joined. "When I first met them, they talked about God's love, how Jesus died to save mankind, and how, if we love God, we should do His work. They never told me I'd be expected to be a prostitute for Jesus, have sex with children, and lie to people on the street by telling them that their donations were going to help drug addicts.'' Carla maintains that she joined the Family of Love with uninformed consent.

Cult recruiters can be found on the streets of our cities, peddling their products or literature and trying to win converts. Recruiters and fund-raisers may be found in airports, at traffic lights, in parking lots, in bus and train stations, on college campuses, in high schools, in prisons and hospitals, in bars and night clubs, at the front door of suburban homes, and even in churches. Sometime, some place, you or a loved one will no doubt be approached by a cultist. The best safeguard against unwitting involvement is to be informed about the recruitment process.

THE LOOK OF LOVE

It is not hard to spot cult recruiters. They generally have a striking appearance. They may seem radiantly happy, but they often wear what psychologist Robert Lifton calls, "thousand-mile stare"—the blank expression in their eyes that does not match their upturned mouth. Or they may appear deeply depressed, with a pallid, undernourished, and fatigued look. These two states are opposite sides to the same coin.

Some ex-members report that the most compelling feature of the recruiter was his or her eyes. "I just couldn't get over their eyes," confesses Pam, an ex-Krishna. "Their gaze was so intense it made me feel naked and vulnerable. I couldn't seem to break their stare and get away ... I felt mesmerized." In the Family of Love, members are taught to unnerve potential converts with what is euphemistically called "the look of love." Their stare is powerful, but, despite allegations of such, we have uncovered no scientific evidence to support the use of hypnosis in cults.

LOVE BOMBING

With the obvious exception of the doomsday cult members, who greet passers-by with "Repent or perish!" the initial approach of a recruiter is generally a soft sell.

Most often a recruiter will approach a potential convert with an optimistic, positive remark. Standing very near the listener, invading "personal space," and looking intently into his or her eyes, the recruiter speaks in glowing but vague terms about his or her faith and "family" which is serving God. Usually it is the person, rather than the sales pitch, that holds the listener's rapt attention.

With effervescent enthusiasm and apparently unfeigned sincerity, the recruiter draws the prospect into a conversation in order to learn his or her personal interests. The listener will be encouraged to visit the recruiter's home or center. At this point the prospective convert may well be unaware that this friendly stranger is connected with a cult, and the recruiter is unlikely to volunteer such information.

Cult recruiters are practically unsurpassed in their ability to spot the lonely and confused and then take advantage of those in such unhappy states. Flattery and ego-stroking are routinely used to gain a potential convert's good will and trust.

The cultic recruitment technique of "love bombing," or ego-stroking, is perfectly designed to condition the prospect to warm empathy with the group. People have a need for self-identity, as well as human solidarity and community. It's no accident that the term "family" and the word "father" turn up again and again in cult literature and speech. People want to belong to something larger than themselves. In this age of alienation and loneliness, the cult rectifies the sense of alienation, and affirms main-line society as corrupt or demonic. Then the cure for loneliness—the attention that must be given to every human being if he or she is to be completely healthy—is heaped upon the prospective convert.

"I always thought I was ugly. I never even believed my husband thought I was beautiful or sexy," the former hooker for the Children of God confesses. "Then these two handsome young men insist that I am beautiful, that I am good and pleasant and worthwhile. I believed them because I *wanted* to believe them.

"When they asked me to leave home and join the group, I went. I would have followed them anywhere and done anything. I did. I did anything I was asked to do."

Often a cult member of the opposite sex will inundate the potential convert with warmth, declarations of love and friendship, and unconditional acceptance and understanding. This unscrupulous sales technique can prove a valuable tool in attracting the vulnerable and the young who have not yet learned that there are no instant friendships.

A GOD-SHAPED VOID

One is reminded of the words of Alfred Edward Housman:

> I, a stranger and afraid
> In a world I never made.

We are all strangers and we are all afraid of many things. Perhaps that's why theologians like Paul Tillich and Karl Barth tell us we are all incurably religious. We are all looking for God or for someone or something we can trust. As Frederich Schleiermacher observed, "Religion is the feeling of absolute dependence." Luther declared, with Paul, that "we live by faith." Sörren Kierkegaard proclaimed that we should make "the leap of faith." And revivalists from John Wesley to Billy Graham have exhorted us to be "born again," become new creatures, and commit ourselves wholly to God. The cultic recruiter has the same message! Only the concrete details are different from the exhortations of the electronic church or the altar call of the Fundamentalist revival: "Bring your needs to the Lord. He will forgive you and make all things right. Only believe, commit, trust.''

CALL TO COMMITMENT

Part of a successful recruiting program involves an appeal to idealism. The call for total commitment to a significant cause stirs something deep within many young people. A potential convert who has been sufficiently attracted by the warmth and friendship of the recruiter is then introduced to the concept of total commitment and made to feel guilty and even fearful of divine retribution if he or she does not follow the example of the cult members who are ''devoting their lives to Christ'' or ''living for God 100 percent.''

Milton C. described his first meeting with the recruiter from the Christian-based cult of which he is a former member: ''These two people seemed tremendously friendly and happy, like no one I'd ever seen before. They asked me about my occupation and my interests—social work and religion. Their warmth and idealism attracted me. They seemed genuinely interested in me and made me feel important by the way they listened intently to everything I had to say. I felt really understood. I was also curious to find out what made them so happy, and to know more about their lifestyle which they praised so profoundly. I didn't know a thing about cults, and I guess that put me at a disadvantage. I accepted their offer to visit their center. That began my three-year involvement.''

"COME ON OVER TO MY HOUSE"

Dr. John Clark, in *Destructive Cult Conversion: Theory, Research, and Treatment,* has described the recruitment process:

> The recruiter controls the flow of information so that he can find out as much about the prospect as quickly as possible and then present the would-be convert with selected bits of information to arouse interest in the

recruiter and the group he represents . . . the proselytiz-ers aim to make the group extremely attractive to the prospect. They touch him deeply with expressions of great concern for his well-being, even with professions of love, and by studied attention to his ideas, interests, and hopes.

The goal is to effect a conversion. This is often accomplished more easily when the potential convert is drawn to the cult's territory. This can take the form of an invitation to dinner or a lecture, a meeting, a Bible study, a self-improvement seminar, or even a weekend retreat. Upon accepting the invitation, the potential convert has no idea that he or she may end up committing life and possessions to this group rather than merely enjoying an evening's social interaction.

COUNTERING RECRUITING TACTICS

After my lectures, I am frequently asked, "What should I do, or advise my children to do, if approached by a cult recruiter?"

Generally I reply that it is a good idea not to talk with them, donate money, or argue. Recruiters are programmed with slick, pat answers to any objections an uninformed person might raise. They are skillfully trained to run confusing, irrational circles around a person with faulty logic and can cite out-of-context Scripture quotations to support a point. Anyone lacking a thorough knowledge of cult strategies should steer clear of cult recruiters.

On the other hand, someone with a thorough knowledge of cults could raise questions that would point up the contradictions in the cult and would plant seeds of doubt in the mind of the member. For example, one might ask: "How can Rev. Moon manufacture munitions in Korea while preaching love? In His Word, God says we should not lie, and yet you lie to people about where their donations are going. How can you justify what you are doing as God's work?''

An act of common human kindness, such as buying a tired and hungry recruiter a sandwich, can counteract the cult's indoctrination that no love exists outside the group. (Contributions of money for food will probably be turned over to the cult.)

Many parents also ask my advice on how they can prevent their children from ever getting involved with a cult. While I cannot offer a foolproof formula, there are several practical actions that may prevent involvement:

1. Parents and children can become educated concerning cults, their characteristics, and their persuasion techniques by reading some of the fine books on cult phenomenon listed in the bibliography and by attending "cult awareness" programs sponsored by churches, schools, and libraries.

2. If the lines of communication between parent and child have been kept open, a child will feel comfortable discussing with his or her parents any chance meeting with a cult recruiter.

3. A young person's knowledge of Christianity and satisfaction in a church's youth activities serve as deterrents to cult involvement.

4. A child who is a questioner and an independent thinker, who possesses ability to reason, will be best equipped to resist a recruiter.

Steve Allen, whose son Brian is a member of the Love Israel cult, notes a dissipation of such skills among Americans in his book *Beloved Son: A Story of the Jesus Cults:*

I believe, in fact, that over the past twenty-five years there has been a steady, demonstrable deterioration of the American intelligence.

. . .Neither we nor our children know how to think, how to reason, how to evaluate logically the arguments of those who want to sell us one bill of goods or another . . . To me, the proliferation of partly mindless belief can be ascribed in large part to ignorance of relevant information and the inability to think well.

Mr. Allen goes on to suggest adding "a fourth 'R' to our formal process of early education. The four would be readin', writin', 'rithmetic, and reasoning."

5. A child who is shown a parent's love, in word as well as in deed, in recognizable and appreciable ways, will be least likely to consider alienating him or herself from such loving parents by affiliating with a destructive cult.

The popular bumper sticker "Have You Hugged Your Child Today?" may strike an uncomfortable note in parents who are caught up in the busy routine of earning a living and running a household. How often we neglect to prove our love to our children!

Countercult activist Rabbi Maurice Davis related quizzing his class of teenagers by secret ballot: What would you most like to ask your parents?

Response after response was: "Do you love me?" "Do you love me?" "Do you love me?"

One thing is certain. The cults will not hesitate to answer that question in the affirmative. They will assure a young person of love and acceptance.

COUNTERING A LOVED ONE'S INTEREST

An individual can be most easily persuaded to reevaluate his decision to become involved in a cult when he or she is teetering on the brink of commitment. At this stage, the cult usually has a strong, manipulative, emotional hold on the individual, but it has deliberately neglected to give him factual information about the group, its leader, beliefs, goals, and cost of commitment. The appeal is to the emotions, not to the mind.

At this point concerned parents might make the following tactful suggestions:

1. "Give yourself some more time before making your decision."

Parents might point out that the child owes it to him or herself and to God to be fully informed about the group before making any commitments. "Several days or weeks to think this over is insignificant compared to a lifetime of membership in this group. Give yourself some time. Think it over. Sleep on it. Talk to others who know more about the group than you do. Then make your decision." This line of reasoning might also be used with a long-term cult member who is experiencing a period of despondency and doubt.

The essence of the reevaluation is helping the potential member take an objective look at the cult, its beliefs, its claims, and the cost of commitment.

2. "Do you know what will be expected of you?"

Several concerned relatives have asked me how to approach their loved ones who were considering joining the Children of God/Family of Love. Drawing on my own experience as a member of that cult, I suggested they present the stark realities of cult experience and strongly urge would-be members to consider the implications, explained throughout this book and in the appendix.

Some of the realities of membership in this cult are that members must engage in prostitution and that cult children are often involved in sexual activity with both adults and peers. Many members avoid accepting the truth of these acts by interpreting them according to David Berg's prosaic mumbo jumbo. Berg has translated prostitution as "showing God's love for the lost," and explains sexual activity with children as fulfilling a God-implanted need within these unfortunate youngsters.

Parents acting as reevaluators must draw aside the shroud of mystic rationalizations and confront the prospective member (their child) with the raw facts.

3. "What does God's Word have to say about the matter?"

Here is an excellent technique for exposing the error of cultic doctrine in the light of biblical truth. Of course, the parents must be informed of cult teachings so as to properly counter them with the correct scriptural interpretation. A minister or theologian might be asked to give assistance.

For example, to a young person interested in the Children of God, one might say, "In the law of Moses, God forbade adultery and incest. Would God contradict Himself by allowing or commanding these activities through your leader, Moses David? Christ said, 'Think not that I have come to abolish the law and the prophets . . . I have come to fulfill them' (Matt. 5:17). How can someone claim to be a godly man if he is destroying the Law?"

4. "Is 'the call' worth what you will have to pay?"

The prospective member should be encouraged to consider the long-term effects of the cult practices and doctrines, and whether or not those consequences could possibly be God's will. Statistics proving such effects could be presented.

The process of confrontation and "reality testing" can be adapted to any destructive cult once there is knowledge of the cult's doctrines and practices.

5. "Whatever you decide, we'll love you still."

In the final analysis, the young person must be allowed to make his or her own decision. If, after having heard the facts, a young person still decides to become a part of the group, it is imperative that family and friends continue to reaffirm their love and support. This action contradicts the insistence of many cults that love does not exist outside of their group and that the world is consumed with selfish interests. It is also a clear example of *agape,* that God-like love that persists in the face of open hostility and rejection.

2. Cult Conditioning: Indoctrination of the Individual

It does not take a loaded gun at the temple to mold a person into being the perfect Moonie, Hare Krishna, or member of the Children of God/Family of Love. All it took for me was a song in the park, an invitation to dinner, and months of clever, centuries-old techniques of persuasion which short-circuited my thinking process and ultimately altered my behavior to conform to the cultic image.

It is in this ability to control a member's thinking and behavior that a cult maintains its power. The Chinese call this process "thought reform." This phrase has been poorly translated into English as the familiar term, "brainwashing."

Contrary to the notion that physical force is a necessary part of thought reform, Dr. Margaret Singer, who has worked with many returning Korean prisoners of war, says, "I know all about the world of gun-at-the-head coercion, prisoner-of-war camps, and the taking of hostages. I just want to tell you that cults can do it better because it's much easier to get people to do your bidding through manipulating their guilt and anxiety and by never directly confronting them and frightening them, but to make their own inner guilt and anxiety change their behavior to fit management's plans."

Thought reform is a process, not an event. Step by step, this process is designed to break a person's independence and individuality and to substitute the characteristics of a pawn. Some of the steps overlap, but they work together to actualize one end—the erasure of self and autonomy to facilitate internal cultic control. For the sake of convenience, the steps have been labeled. Many of them have been documented by Dr. Robert J. Lifton, associate professor of psychiatry at Yale University, in his book *Thought Reform and the Psychology of Totalism*. This study has become the standard by which to judge whether or not a group is "brainwashing" its recruits.

Groups should be judged, case by case, according to the number of abusive behavior modification techniques employed. The utilization of all or most of these techniques would indicate intentional thought reform and would distance the group from other organizations that employ but do not abuse behavior modification techniques.

Among the groups most commonly defined as major destructive cults are: the Unification church (the Moonies), the Divine Light Mission, the Children of God/Family of Love, the International Society for Krishna Consciousness (Hare Krishna), the Way International, the Church of Bible Understanding (the Forever Family), the Love Family (the Church of Armageddon), the Church of Scientology, and the Body of Christ (the Body). (See the appendix for full descriptions of many destructive cults).

THE DESTRUCTIVE PROCESS: CONTROL OVER ENVIRONMENT AND TIME

The destructive cult gains control over a member's environment and time by having the member live in or spend all free time with the group. In these situations the cult can exert tremendous power over what is seen, heard, and experienced. For example, many cults monitor all information from the outside world. Books, magazines, newspapers, TV, and radio are either banned or viewed with skepticism. By day and often well into the night, new members of many cults are bombarded with the group's teachings and ideology through marathon classes, lectures, and reading. In some live-in groups, tapes of the doctrines are played while members are arising, retiring, sleeping, and performing routine chores. Eventually, it is believed, the member will be completely indoctrinated and under the control of the "savior."

Cults often control the contacts and relationships a member enjoys on the outside, and this control is rigidly enforced at the beginning of the member's involvement.

THE DESTRUCTIVE PROCESS: MANIPULATION OF THE ENVIRONMENT

Cult members are often kept in a frenzy of activity, leaving no time or energy to reflect upon what is happening to them. These activities are usually cult-related—fund raising, proselytizing, group rituals, study of cult doctrine, and so forth.

While on a mobile fund-raising team, Benji, an ex-Moonie quoted in Josh Freed's *Moonwebs: Journey into the Mind of a Cult,* spent eighteen hours a day selling flowers on the streets "sleeping as little as one hour a night and eating almost nothing." Most cults force their members to maximum productivity.

Cult life abounds with contrived spontaneity designed to appear mysterious, divine, and powerful. Ex-Moonie Erica concurred with this statement when she spoke of a weekend retreat held by her cult: "Heart-warming moments (such as weeping during testimonials) . . . had all been planned beforehand to look spontaneous.

Such peak or ecstatic experiences are engineered to reinforce a convert's commitment, both to the cult and to the abandonment of self. The peak experience often occurs in a group setting when the entire group is engaging in chanting, speaking in tongues, ecstatic singing, dancing, and clapping. After prolonged engagement in these activities, the group can reach a drug-like high and some members may experience euphoria, dizziness, lack of sensation in the body, hysteria, hallucinations, and the hearing of voices. A vivid example is a ceremony of the Hare Krishna which Flo Conway and Jim Siegelman describe in an article entitled "Information Disease: Have the Cults Created a New Mental Illness?'' which appeared in *Science Digest* (January 1982). In the Hare Krishna's *arti ka* ceremony, new recruits, led by older members, perform a feverish, jumping dance amid flickering lights, heavy incense, loud, droning music and pounding drums until they are physically and emotionally overcome.''

The information fed a new recruit is generally orchestrated to trigger a "revelation" about the group and its leader. Suggestions about the divine stature of the leader and the group are frequently planted in the member's mind, especially during the suggestive state following a peak experience. This is done through taking Bible verses out of context, misconstruing world events and the alleged "revelations" of the leader himself. Pressured by the faith of other members and enlightened veterans, the member may, in time, yield to the power of suggestion. In this "moment of truth," he or she makes the required leap of faith to embrace the cultic doctrine.

"No one ever told me outright that Moon was the Messiah," said Jim, an ex-Moonie. "They didn't have to. Based on the information they gave me, it was self-evident. After several months in the group, things began falling in place like a jigsaw puzzle. All the signposts pointed to Moon being the Lord of the Second Advent: that a messiah, like Jesus, was walking the earth; that his time and place of birth coincided with Moon's; that the world was ripe for a savior. One day it just clicked . . . I realized Moon was that Messiah!"

Once the member believes in the divine status of the leader and his mission, he must also accept that the teachings are holy and above question. This leads to a great ideological polarization. Either the member is "with God" (in agreement with the leader) or "against God," and siding with Satan. Consequently, any contradictions and inconsistencies seen in the leader and his teachings must be rationalized and suppressed.

"I couldn't understand how Maharaji Ji (leader of the

Divine Light Mission) could eat McDonald's hamburgers after telling us that we must be vegetarians," observed ex-member Marcia. "I had to rationalize the contradiction by telling myself that he was above the law. He was spiritual enough to eat meat—it wouldn't contaminate him. On the other hand, we weren't spiritual enough. Also we had been taught that God was playing games with us through such contradictions in order to break our old, worldly concepts. Maharaji Ji played with our heads like this to make us believe that nothing made any sense and that we couldn't trust our rational minds."

Many cult leaders live in material luxury, if not opulence, at the expense of their followers. The principal cults are fond of saying: "From each according to his ability, to each according to his need." These high-sounding words are distorted and the basis for rationalization by the members—just as Marcia rationalized the guru's breach of vegetarianism: The leaders are spiritually mature or deserving enough to enjoy these material blessings, while their followers are not.

Cults continually single out an enemy to keep doubts at bay and the members fighting for purity of thought. Satan or evil is personified in everything outside the group, even other cults. In their early days, the Children of God conducted guerrilla attacks on other Jesus people and churches by deliberately disrupting services. As a rule the member's world is reduced to two black-and-white principles: God (the leader) and the Devil (everything and everyone outside the sphere of the leader and his followers). Satan can be blamed for everything that opposes the member or the group. Satan allegedly rules the world outside the cult, and the members are engaged in a life-and-death struggle with him. This polarization leads to a siege mentality and sometimes to a state of spiritual paranoia. Since Satan is responsible for the member's old concepts, thoughts, and feelings, they should be, must be repressed;

the real self, mind, and emotions of the member are vilified as the enemy.

Father Kent Burtner, O.P., an Oregon priest who has counseled many ex-members, criticizes this narrow frame of reference: "Any belief system that so polarized good and bad is intellectually dishonest . . . and denies the value of the human person. I am sick unto death of those kids being so exploited."

THE DESTRUCTIVE PROCESS: EMPHASIS ON INDIVIDUAL GUILT

Many cults require that new members participate in confessional or "sharing" sessions, either in a group or with a few select leaders or veterans. Here the leaders may cull sensitive information about the convert that can be used later to manipulate him or her into staying in the cult.

These intense sessions are also designed to dredge up old conflicts and problems and thus provoke a spiritual identity crisis. As past short-comings are admitted, the convert is encouraged to become deeply introspective and question the very fundamentals of his or her life. This is a type of induced crisis, which is exacerbated by ecstatic peak periods and other manipulative techniques.

In the words of noted cult expert, Dr. John Clark, "The key to mind control is the maintenance of this state of dissociation for a significant period, so that in this state of extended emergency, the victim must identify with the captor."

Usually a new member is conditioned to accept the concept that everything and everyone in his or her past life is bad and must be abandoned. Allegedly the member's life has only been godly since joining the group. This gives rise to the "prodigal son" syndrome that exists in many cults, where the member is encouraged to exaggerate the wickedness of precult life. This reinforces the idea that the group "saves" its members from evil, and it makes defection unthinkable and even terrifying. The more the convert decries the past, the more he or she becomes isolated from it. The convert begins to live only in the immediate world of the cult.

Guilt is a powerful tool in the hands of those who would exploit it, and all humans can be vulnerable to this manipulation. Thought reform expert Dr. Robert J. Lifton maintains that "There is tremendous stress upon individual guilt (in cults) and since we all have a store of guilt or potential guilt, our guilt can be tapped." Most cults strive to assert a stranglehold of guilt within its members—guilt over past sins, thinking of something other than the group and its ideology, sexual sins, guilt over never working hard enough for the cause, for entertaining doubts or questions, or even for thinking rationally and analytically about the group. This list is long and reaches to the point of absurdity. For instance, members of the Children of God were made to feel guilty for using dental floss and for boiling cabbage—activities that, according to the leader David Berg, were outside the will of God.

The blame for any misfortune or illness is usually laid at the feet of the member and imputed to an individual's lack of faith. This day-to-day maintenance of guilt by shrewd cult leaders is essential to the control of the member.

THE DESTRUCTIVE PROCESS: DEPRIVATION AND ABUSE

Lack of sleep, inadequate food and clothing, little privacy, and inferior medical attention are commonplace in many cults. Often a cult demands that a person surrender all possessions and money to the group with the understanding that the group will supply all personal daily needs. But personal needs of "average" members are often met skimpily, if at all.

Although the diet in some groups is nutritionally adequate, albeit inexpensive, in others it is plainly deficient. Proteins, especially meats, are the most expensive foods, and expenses must generally be held down to allow as much money as possible to be channeled into the work or sent directly to the leadership.

Barbara L., who was in charge of buying food for a Divine Light Mission ashram (house) in the middle seventies, recalls that her food budget was limited to a dollar per person per day. "That meant a lot of starch and not much protein," she said. (The leader of this group, Guru Maharaji Ji, is one of the most ostentatiously wealthy of the cult leaders.)

Some groups do not even meet this meager standard. One nomadic group known as "the garbage eaters" scavenge their daily fare from dumpsters behind restaurants and stores.

Many groups limit sleep in an effort to allow more time for cult-related work and indoctrination. The need for sleep is frequently regarded as a spiritual weakness, and those who make do with a few hours of rest are lauded as spiritually superior to those who can't manage as well. In both the Unification church and the Family of Love, fatigue is labeled as "an attack of sleep demons" and thought to be largely unrelated to physiological causes. In some cults the only sleeping facilities provided are the floor and sleeping bags. The pressure to exceed one's capacity for cult work is often severe. Long hours of fund-raising coupled with scant sleep can, in time, deplete a person's physical and mental resources. Privacy is at a premium in many live-in groups. Generally, space costs money. Many members live in overcrowded conditions with no space to call their own. Deprivation in cults is of heightened concern when if affects children. Lack of food and medical attention, in particular, are more menacing to children than to adults. But sometimes deprivation goes beyond the shortage of physical necessities. Some groups, acting on the belief that schools are satanic, deny their children even the most rudimentary education. Some other groups separate parents and children, sending the offspring to be raised in a cult nursery or school. In one poignant documentary, young Hare Krishna children attested, in voices hoarse from continuous chanting, that they knew neither their mother nor their father. These same children were later seen eating off the floor and taking cold showers. The line between discipline and abuse is sometimes crossed. According to some ex-members of the Body cult, many of their children and infants are severely beaten several times a day. The beatings are administered to "break the will and individuality." One ex-member observed that these children were not allowed to play, but spent all their time working.

In the Family of Love, many of the children are subjected to sexual exploitation. The leader's writings encourage adult masturbation of children, favor incest, and promote childhood intercourse. Sexual abuse also marked life with the People's Temple.

Deprivation and abuse foster submission to cultic control on the part of the cult member, whether adult or child.

THE DESTRUCTIVE PROCESS: DEMOTION FROM ADULT STATUS

In the outside world, adults and adolescents are viewed as just that—adults and adolescents. In a cult, the new member generally is viewed by the group as a newborn baby. The rationale behind this stripping of identity is simple: A newcomer to the truth must be reeducated correctly in cultic ways. This vulnerable, childlike status essentially delivers the convert into the hands of the leaders for molding. The new recruit must abandon the precepts and lessons learned in his precult life and look to the already enlightened—the leaders and veterans of the cult—for all guidance, direction, and truth.

Part of the new convert's commitment to God is to work toward becoming a "disciple" or "godly person" by following the blueprint of the cult. A commitment to improve oneself is commendable, but within a destructive cult, this commitment translates into the erasure of one's own precultic self, integrity, character, and personality in favor of the super-imposition of the cult personality.

"We were out to change the world," said one ex-member of an Eastern cult, "but first we had to change ourselves. That meant letting go of all our old values and adopting the standards of the group. We were completely at the whim of the leader and what he decreed to be 'good' at any particular time. 'Good' or 'God's will' really meant whatever served our leader best. So it was 'moral' to lie and short-change people while fund-raising because we were collecting their money for God. It was 'honest' to conceal our true identity from a potential convert until we had him or her well hooked. 'Good' was defined as devoting ourselves to God in strict obedience to His will—which in reality meant obeying our leader implicitly."

The ugly catch in what otherwise would seem an idealistic commitment to self-improvement is that the new convert has no idea where these character changes will lead—whether it be to a sleazy bar, offering his or her body to potential converts, or to a jungle in Guyana. Yet, submission to the radical personality changes demanded by the cult is perceived as an act of strength, a surrender to the workings of God—not to the manipulations of man.

3. Religious Totalism: Control of the Individual

"You must give yourself completely to Jesus and His new King David!" shrieked the puffy-faced local cult leader. "God's anointed leader, Moses David (David Berg), says that we must show God's love to the lowliest person, for 'whatsoever you do to the least of these my brethren, you do unto me.' That means you must even be willing to have sexual relations with anyone you meet in order to persuade him or her of God's love and to win that person as a new convert. Hallelujah!"

Sooner or later, the leader's teachings are venerated as absolute truths that may take precedence over moral or secular laws. In most cases, the words and writings of this cultic leader are considered superior to the Scriptures. David Brandt Berg (Moses David of the Children of God) says it is better to read his "MO"letters than the Bible, for the Bible was the Word of God for yesterday, while *his* letters are the Word of God for today. No matter how irrational or repugnant a teaching, (such as Moses David's declaration of religious prostitution), it must be welcomed, believed, absorbed, and obeyed because it is allegedly divine.

A member who fails to accept a teaching will be shamed, punished, or even excommunicated. In my observations, this shaming process was typified by the Children of God. Anyone who couldn't accept Moses David's new revelations, particularly "flirty fishing" (religious prostitution as promulgated in diatribes such as the above mentioned exhortation by a local cult leader), was labeled a weak brother or sister. This was the ultimate humiliation, equal to being branded a backslider or traitor. It was a public announcement that one was failing God. Rejection of a teaching could mean expulsion from the group and a return to Satan's world.

THE DESTRUCTIVE PROCESS: CONTROL OF LANGUAGE

Many cults have their own version of "non-thought language." Some words and terms have come to have meanings other than the commonly accepted usage.

Like Orwellian "newspeak," cultic language is designed to diminish rather than expand the member's range of thought and base of reference. For instance, the word "good" in most cults does not mean what is moral, but what is best for the group. "Truth" comes to mean whatever the leader says. "Love" is used to justify acts of the group, no matter how cruel, such as hiding members from their disapproving families. It is interesting to note that Charles Manson's women killed for "love."

An extreme example of cultic language control took place in the Alaskan branch of the Body cult. There, children were forbidden to use the personal pronouns "me" and "mine," supposedly to prevent the development of any sense of personal identity.

Most cultic language control is not so extreme. However, when a newly indoctrinated member speaks with the family back home, they may not be able to understand this new "language." The confusion and lack of comprehension that results will only reinforce what the group leaders have been saying—that a great gulf of alienation exists between true believers and the outside world.

Cult members operate on a fifth-grade-level philosophy and theology built of thought-terminating clichés. Complex situations are reduced to brief bromides which, according to Dr. Robert Lifton, "are the beginning and end of any kind of discourse."

Said ex-member Rich: "There was a lot of packaging . . .

people were reduced to clichés. People outside our group were called 'systemites.' "

Rational questions and apprehensions about the group are habitually labeled "the voice of the Devil." According to Dr. John Clark, language skills dissipate within many cults to the point where the members "lose the use of metaphor, mirth, and irony."

Some cults adopt certain religious words and terminology for the purpose of camouflaging themselves as accepted main-line religions. David Berg calls himself "Father David," although he is not an ordained priest. Unification church members often pass themselves off during fundraising activities as a "Christian interdenominational youth group," though any Christian theologian will affirm that a belief in Rev. Moon as the Messiah in no way constitutes orthodox Christianity. This kind of manipulation and usurpation of religious terminology is an effort to make the group appear acceptable to the uninformed.

THE DESTRUCTIVE PROCESS: IDEOLOGY OVER REALITY

Within the first six months, the convert's commitment to the cult usually shifts from an emotional attachment to a powerful intellectual one. The essence of this commitment is the renouncing of oneself to "God"—meaning, for most cult members, the cult leader. An example of this suppression of personal feelings is the common cult dictum that the members must appear happy and enthusiastic at all times in order to convince outsiders of the value of the group and to reinforce the commitment of the other members. This happiness must be affected and the enthusiasm studied if a cult member lacks these feelings. In effect, personal feelings of ambivalence are overriden in favor of the cult ideology.

Ignoring any reality that does not coincide with group ideology can have serious consequences in the area of health. A number of groups hold that sickness and accidents are results of sin and should be prayed away. The danger arises when a member ignores, or is denied medical attention as a "sign of faith." Many cults are reluctant to pay for even the most routine medical attention.

I encountered one such case when I was with the Children of God in Scandinavia. Finding a Danish sister crying bitterly, I knew immediately that something was seriously wrong—such a display of emotion was taboo. She confided to me that she had a severe case of VD, which our leader blamed on lack of faith. The leader had declared that her going to a doctor would be a sign of spiritual weakness. When her condition worsened despite prayer, Ruth telephoned her mother, who insisted on taking her to and paying for a doctor. Our leader reprimanded Ruth for her treachery in calling for help on the "outside." However, shortly thereafter, Ruth left with her mother and never returned. We were told that she was just a "weak sister," unsuitable for God's army.

Believing in cult ideology to the exclusion of reality can lead a member to rationalize those untruths and deceptions that are in line with group doctrine. Some cults employ deception on the premise that the end justifies the means, such as bogus healing services to boost the congregation's faith and the pastor's revenue. Some cults label such group-sanctioned practices as "transcendental trickery" and "heavenly deception." The Hare Krishnas, with members disguised as Santa Claus, have been known to raise funds at Christmas. Unification church fund-raisers have masqueraded as cripples to play on the sympathies of potential donors.

Recently, outside a restaurant in Akron, Ohio, an acquaintance of mine, and ex-Moonie himself, became so outraged by this form of deception that he grabbed a "cripple's" flowers and ran down the street. To the amazement of the passers-by, the "cripple" sprang from his wheelchair and sprinted down the street in pursuit!

Placing ideology above reality is motivated by the

member's love of God or idealism. However, this unwitting commitment to the eradication of the member's own self, integrity, and intellect in favor of the cult leader, is as nefarious a concept as self-immolation.

THE DESTRUCTIVE PROCESS: THOUGHT-STOPPING

Nearly all cults deal a terminal blow to the member's fractured self through the enforcing of "self-hypnosis" or "special dissociative" thought-stopping. These thought-stopping techniques, which vary with the cult, can take the form of chanting, meditating, repeating Bible verses or religious phrases, or speaking in tongues. When practiced outside a cult setting, these techniques can be harmless or, as some think, even beneficial. Within a cult framework, however, they are used to inhibit thinking and internalize cultic control. Because the mind is evil, all analytical, rational thinking must be actively suppressed. The member is taught to use these thought-stopping techniques whenever doubts, questions, memories, or emotions arise that are not in line with group ideology.

As one ex-member put it: "We were told that when our old selves emerged, or we started to doubt, think, question, or even feel emotions prohibited by the group, it was Satan trying to seduce us from the truth. We were to smash the voice of the Devil with our chanting. What we were actually doing was short-circuiting our minds."

Frequently a member is told that his or her doubts arise from partial knowledge of the "truth" embraced by the group. Partial truth is untrustworthy and even dangerous. Such a member must wait passively for the "whole truth" to be revealed. This "truth" is fed piecemeal, and by the the time the convert is fully informed, he or she may have become so enmeshed with the group that leaving is difficult, if not inconceivable.

THE DESTRUCTIVE PROCESS: THE DISPENSING OF EXISTENCE

Dr. Robert J. Lifton, in *Thought Reform and the Psychology of Totalism,* speaks of "the dispensing of existence." He writes: "The totalist environment draws a sharp line between those whose right to exist can be recognized, and those who possess no such right."

In general, cult leaders claim to know who should exist and who is not worthy to exist. The innate value of the human being is discounted and a person's value is measured by his or her belief in and use to the cult. The only justification for the existence of outsiders, even family, is the possibility of their conversion and subsequent use to the group. However, an outsider would be considered useful if he or she donated money or goods to the group, or held a position of importance in the community which could be used to influence others in favor of the cult.

In destructive cults, the cause is far more important than the members. The goals of the leader, usually proselytizing and fundraising, are enshrined as the Holy Cause, and the needs, welfare and rights of the members, only secondary considerations.

When I was with the Children of God, I observed a sick infant who was kept out on the streets in the depth of a Scandinavian winter so her parents could reach their fundraising quota. Her medical condition worsened, but only after she had contracted whooping cough were her parents excused from taking her out with them while they solicited funds.

THE DESTRUCTIVE PROCESS: THE GOAL

The sins of the cults are grievous—aborting a young person's personality before it is fully formed, and inhibiting an adult's capacity for rational thought. The ultimate goal of cultic thought reform is self-indoctrination—the internalization of the authority of the leader. This final state is summed up in these words from the Unification Church's 120-day training manual: "I must deny my way of thinking, my way of feeling, my way of talking, everything. My desire, my hope, my joy, my will must be placed on the altar and given to God . . . nothing belongs to myself anymore. . ."

Josh Freed, award-winning author of the book *Moon-webs,* likens cult initiation and training programs to a psychotherapist gone mad. "Like some kind of therapy, Boonville [a Unification Church indoctrination center similar in many respects to other cults' training centers] creates an intense emotional environment that pushes the 'patient' into the recesses of his own mind."

Physical and emotional isolation from family and the outside world, mental and physical deprivation, manipulative techniques, and the new recruit's ignorance of such "therapeutic" methods all intensify the effectiveness of the cult's thought reform program. The convert's defenses are broken down with remarkable speed. Unlike ethical psychotherapists, cult programmers do not lead a person to look inwardly for solutions and answers, but "close in, deliberately using the recruit's growing vulnerability to drive him to the very brink of a nervous breakdown." According to Freed, the cult then offers itself as the weakened recruit's only salvation, asking in return abdication of inner self and complete submission to the group. The "therapist" becomes the devourer who preys on his unwitting victim.

The eventual loss experienced by the convert can be devastating. In the words of Dr. Lifton: "One can seem to have a free will in that, at that point, one does not have a gun to one's head and one is not being directly coerced. But one has lost the capacity for independent thought, independent and free imagination. That's losing a lot."

4. Walking Out and Breaking Free

Defection from a destructive cult, whether voluntary or involuntary, can be extremely difficult. The psychological conditioning and pressures to conform to cult expectations make defection difficult, although not impossible, in the majority of cases.

VOLUNTARY EXIT

Sociological studies point to a high voluntary turnover rate in most cults, up to seventy-five percent annually according to at least one nationwide survey of the Unification Church. According to Dick Anthony, psychologist and former research coordinator of the Center for the Study of New Religions at the Graduate Theological Union, Berkeley, California: "There is a consensus among scholars of these groups that they [the cults] have a substantial voluntary turnover rate."

A large number of members walked out of the Divine Light Mission when the Guru, who advocated celibacy, married his secretary. Others left when the Millennium did not visibly start, as predicted. Many defected from the Children of God/Family of Love after Berg instituted prostitution. Though the number of voluntary defectors from cults is almost impossible to validate, two sociologists, David G. Bromley and Anson D. Shupe, authors of the book *Strange Gods,* have also estimated the rate of turnover in most cults to be quite large.

The fact that cult members can and do walk out of cults on their own testifies to the fact that, though conditioned by the cult, members' conditioning is not so complete as to render them mindless robots. Some factors that can lead to voluntary defection are: developing maturity, disillusionment, growing doubts about the cult, dissatisfaction with cult life, and the emotional pull of loved ones left behind.

DEVELOPING MATURITY

The urge to separate from one's parents is a normal phase of growing up. A young person who encounters a cult recruiter during this rebellious phase of his life could be persuaded to express his independence by opposing his family and joining a countermovement.

Though this young person may have met a short-sighted goal, his or her progressive needs for personal independence and autonomy cannot be met within the totalitarian structure of a cult. Eventually such a person will feel stifled, act on this growing dissatisfaction, and simply leave, having "outgrown" the group.

DISILLUSIONMENT

In millennial groups, disillusionment is inevitable. As the prophecies and predictions of the leaders fail to materialize, as the heralded utopian age never arrives, the sincere believer becomes the disillusioned believer.

Steve Kemperman, a one-time Moonie, recounts his disenchantment in his book, *Lord of the Second Advent:* "I'd been . . . talking to old colleagues from my Oakland and early (cult) days . . . I had known them when they were fairly young members, excited about the movement, hopeful and sparky. Now they looked out at me through sad, tired hound-dog eyes. During those young-old days all of us believed we'd be halfway to the Kingdom of Heaven by 1977! The entire Family did! Now in 1977 we simply *endured* our mission, like men chew on dry, stringy meat . . . My heart and mind seemed stranded on a stale, joyless desert, like withering dying cattle."

Disillusionment can also be fueled by a cult's extreme demands. Some members leave because they tire of

Dealing With Destructive Cults

marathon fundraising, or the ever-increasing financial demands of some groups that sell their "truth" in courses. My own disillusionment with the Children of God/ Family of Love passed the point of no return when sexual activity with children and prostitution were advocated. My fear for the mental and emotional health of my two young sons gave me the courage to leave the cult, thereby sparing them from any such abuse.

GROWING DOUBTS AND DISSATISFACTION

It can be reasonably assumed that all cult members have doubts at one time or another. Despite the implementation of thought-stopping techniques, doubts about the leader and his message often take root and grow.

Family and friends can assist the growth of doubts and of the likelihood of defection by staying in communication with the cult member, being sensitive to the signs of disillusionment. At those times it is possible to introduce concepts and raise questions that stimulate doubt and promote rational thought.

A cult member who is not fortunate enough to have family and friends who encourage doubt about the cult may have misgivings adequately aggravated by the day-to-day realities of the cult and its life style. For example, a young mother, with membership in a cult that stresses faith healing and scorns medical attention, might leave the cult when faced with the reality of a seriously ill child, particularly if the child's condition has not improved with prayer. In such a case, most cults would recognize that the usefulness or potential usefulness of a truly sick member had ceased, and would abandon him, whether child or adult. Most groups are loath to pay for medical attention or admit the need for such attention, fearing a serious blow to their invincibility and control over members' lives. I have never heard of a communal cult that provides medical insurance for members who depend on the group for their livelihood.

For some members, these gnawing doubts lead to a moment of truth. Such was the case with Philip P., an ex-Divine Light Mission member, who said, "After several years it just came to me . . . Guru Maharaji Ji couldn't be God. How could God be such a jerk?"

Humans are basically rational beings who gravitate toward that which gives pleasure and retreat from that which causes pain. As long as a cult membership provides positive benefits, the member will be inclined to stay. But when the cost of these benefits becomes too demanding or painful, the member will be motivated to withdraw.

EMOTIONAL PULL

A destructive cult destroys or sabotages the member's natural family ties. Often, out-of-context Scripture passages are used to rationalize this cruel severance:

> "For I have come to set a man against his father, and a daughter against her mother, and a daughter-in-law against her mother-in-law; and a man's foes will be those of his own household. He who loves father or mother more than me is not worthy of me; and he who loves son or daughter more than me is not worthy of me" (Matt. 10:35–37).

To an individual unschooled in correct interpretation and the context of these and similar texts, a cult can present a convincing argument that Christ literally meant for His disciples (past and present) to turn against their own flesh-and-blood. Other passages such as the commandment to honor your father and mother and Christ's own example of tender consideration toward His mother, are not considered in this kind of proof-texting.

"We were taught that our parents were demons," said one defector from an Eastern cult. "We were told that they were only interested in the animal activities of eating, sleeping, and sex; while we, on the other hand, were striving toward godliness and purity. We had to rid ourselves of our parents and their evil influence lest they contaminate us also."

At one time during my five-year membership in the Children of God/Family of Love, I showed too much affection for my parents. As a result, I was subjected to days of intensive, intimidating, and humiliating "counseling" sessions staged by the leaders to correct my "spiritual problem." The sessions were continued until I capitulated and, at least outwardly, renounced my parents. In reality, I never severed my emotional ties with them and it was this constant connection that eventually helped me leave the cult.

The "connectedness" with loved ones on the outside is often a lifesaver. How unfortunate that its importance is sometimes underestimated by a member's family.

LEAVE THEM ALONE AND THEY WILL COME HOME?

Exactly what can a family do to encourage a cult member to "come home?" What if the occasional letter or visit is heavy with condemnation, criticism, and outright hostility, and the once loving and dutiful child or mate is scarcely recognizable in this sullen, defiant cult convert?

It is difficult not to feel rejection, humiliation, bewilderment, fear, even anger and disgust. "After all we have done. . ."

But the family should be aware of the power that lies dormant in their connection with their cult-estranged loved one. They must remember that the venomous antifamily rhetoric may not coincide with the cult member's real feelings. In reality the loved one may feel guilty about the pain inflicted upon the family. Unless there were serious problems in the family relationships prior to the cult involvement, it would be reasonable to assume that deep down, the average cult member still cares for his or her family.

This is a time when family and friends should make a

special effort to renew and strengthen relationships with the cult member. The family can maximize their emotional clout in several ways:

1. *Don't argue with a new cultist,* for that is to fight on the wrong battlefield. The convert wasn't reasoned into the cult, so it isn't likely that he or she can be argued out of it. Attacking beliefs or new friends will only make the new convert defensive and determined to embrace the practices of this new religion even more fiercely than might otherwise be the case. No one wants to admit making a serious mistake.

2. *Nurture valid doubts and misgivings about the cult.* The average cult member will have periods of faltering faith about many aspects of the cult. Wise family members and friends will seize these opportunities to point out contradictions and absurdities of the group, thus helping to promote rational thought. This may be the time to introduce factual information about the cult, its unsavory aspects and manipulative techniques.

3. *Bide your time.* Just because someone doesn't change today does not mean there is no hope for the future. A person is lured into—or willingly joins—a cult out of a felt need. Once the need that made the cult seem attractive is met, it is very likely that the person will move on, both psychologically and socially, to another need. Since this higher level of development will be frustrated due to the conformist, authoritarian nature of the average cult, the cult itself will become a new problem. Most of the ex-cultists who left voluntarily expressed unhappiness with the group when it restricted their growth. At that point the conscious mind can begin to perceive that cult leaders and fellow members do, indeed, have feet of clay.

4. *Remain sensitive to signs that your help is wanted.* Suggest subtly that you are always available whenever needed. This advice rests on the premise that the person who enters the cult eventually shakes off some—or all—of the heavy "conditioning" accomplished in cult recruitment

Dealing With Destructive Cults

and indoctrination. As long as the cultist chants, pray-reads, speaks in tongues, meditates, or performs other exercises designed to throw the mind out of gear, he or she may not become sufficiently aware of inner needs. However, dozens of witnesses have testified that they automatically reduced or practically abandoned those practices as time went by.

5. *Continue to affirm love for and commitment to the loved one.* As mentioned before, the unconditional love of the family is a powerful anticult weapon. Keep the channels of communication open, even if the member is hostile. Constantly remind the convert that you love and miss him or her. You want reconciliation. You are only as far away as the nearest telephone. If your loved one should want to come home, a prepaid ticket will be waiting. Being assured of these things can make the long journey back less difficult.

WHILE THERE IS LIFE, THERE IS HOPE

Of course the research cited at the beginning of this chapter is precious little comfort to the family of a long-term member. Nevertheless, for an average cult member, developing maturity, growing doubts, dissatisfaction with cult life, and the emotional pull of loved ones left behind gnaws at cult commitment. After a period of time fanaticism may collapse and he or she may relinquish loyalty and simply walk away. I did.

At a reception held after the release of my autobiography, *Not For a Million Dollars,* a woman approached me with tears in her eyes. "Thank you for writing your story," she said. "You have given hope to many, many parents—hope that their children can someday walk away from a cult. The very fact that you could leave on your own is proof that all things are possible."

NETWORKING

"Our daughter had been in the Moonies for two years before we discovered a parents' group," said one mother. "It was a great relief to meet other parents who were in the same position as we were. Although we would never get our girl deprogrammed, the support that comes from knowing that we are not alone has helped ease this very difficult time."

Many parents have responded to their children's cult involvement by forming a countercult network with a small number of mental health professionals and lawyers in leadership roles. These nationwide networks serve the family that has been touched by cult involvement in at least four ways: As a support system for ex-members and their families; as an information referral system concerned with cults, deprogramming, and rehabilitation; as a public educational arm on cult matters; and as a lobbying arm for anticult legislation. Groups within the network place their emphasis on different functions.

Some Christian-based countercult organizations, such as Spiritual Counterfeits of California, have a doctrinal perspective and, in general, do not condone deprogramming. They are also less involved in political anticult activities than the parental-based groups.

THE HISTORY OF THE COUNTERCULT MOVEMENT

It is generally agreed that the first of the modern anticult groups—"The Parents' Committee to Free Our Sons and Daughters from the Children of God Organization"—was founded in 1971 in San Diego. Its title was soon shortened to "Free the Children of God" (FREECOG).

FREECOG, together with other grassroot anticult groups, tried to counteract the cults through local authorities, such as police, district attorneys, and state bureaucracies, but met with only limited success.

By the middle seventies, the first of several coordinating national organizations was formed. Grassroot groups such as Love Our Children, Inc.; Citizens Engaged in Reuniting Families, Inc.; Return to Personal Choice; and Free Minds, Inc. sprang up. Fueled by a lack of response from local authorities, these anticult associations began voicing their grievances at a federal level—to officials, bureaucrats, and members of Congress. Although the lobbying efforts resulted in two information-gathering hearings conducted by Senator Robert Dole (Kansas) and in several proposals for anticult legislation, no meaningful or decisive action for the parents and against the cults ever took place. Why? Because of concern for religious liberty and the separation of church and state. (See Appendix F).

In October 1976, after several abortive attempts to form one national organization, the anticult associations created the still-operant Citizen Freedom Foundation—Information Services (CFF-IS) to coordinate the nationwide local groups.

Despite the countercult movement's sincere motives and sympathetic and untiring labor, the movement has several liabilities with which to contend: lack of consensus on what exactly constitutes a cult; disagreement over the morality of and need for coercive deprogramming; and the unconstitutionality of some proposed legislation and activities associated with the movement. You will want to check out any association with whom you identify to establish whether or not you agree with their definitions and stands.

5. Kidnapping and Deprogramming

Deprogramming is one of the most controversial aspects of the destructive cult phenomenon. Proponents hail it as a lifesaver of brainwashed cult victims and a new therapy that "frees the mind." Those in opposition claim it is a crime against religious and civil liberties, a kind of spiritual gang rape that should not be condoned by a free society. To learn the truth about deprogramming, we must examine its premise, its process, and its implications for the "prisoners" it proposes to "free."

"LET OUR CHILDREN GO"

Deprogramming, a word coined by Ted Patrick, the pioneer of the process, is forced reevaluation and reconciliation in which coercion and emotion play important roles. One deprogrammer explained it as "showing the cult member the other side" (whether he or she wants to see it or not, we might add). Ted Patrick describes it as "opening up a person's mind so that something other than the programming of the cult can go in for the first time in so many days, weeks, months, or years."

Although the term "deprogramming" is also used to define noncoercive processes, the term shall be used here strictly to refer to coercive measures.

The controversy surrounding deprogramming frequently revolves around the methods employed. Sometimes the process amounts to kidnapping, an illegal act. Once the member has been taken from the cult setting through abduction or trickery, he or she is then involuntarily held—typically in a basement or an obscure motel room.

There the member is subjected to intense emotional sessions in which unsavory facts about the cult, perhaps hitherto unknown to the cult member, are presented. The cultist must answer questions that force him or her to examine critically and realistically the group and its doctrines and practices. The deprogrammer's team includes several "security guards"—usually brawny males—who will, if necessary, restrain the member forcibly from walking away from an unpleasant confrontation.

"Before I can make him talk, I've got to make him feel something . . . and fear is the primal feeling," says deprogrammer Ford Greene.

The deprogrammer attempts to elicit an emotional response from the member, provoking an argumentative discussion. Some deprogrammers use tactics of intimidation or ridicule which might include: shouting, name-calling, or drawing horns on photographs of the cult leader. Ironically a deprogramming cannot work unless there is rapport and exchange—even if negative—between the cult member and the deprogrammer.

A skilled deprogrammer knows how to establish that rapport, arouse the member's emotions, and spot chinks of doubt and weakness in cultic armor. For some members the messianic or infallible status of the leader may be an area of doubt; another may feel guilty for the grief caused his or her family. For the latter, the sight of weeping parents might heavily weight a decision to reevaluate his or her commitment, particularly if the child has been uncertain of the parents' love and concern. Proof of their love is now clearly evident in the effort, expense, and risk they have taken to bring about this reunion.

"RESCUING" CULT VICTIMS

Dozens of ex-cultists interviewed for this book testify to the fact that they did, indeed, benefit from coercive deprogramming. They are grateful that their parents intervened in their lives.

"I can't thank my parents enough," said Josh, a deprogrammed Moonie. "I don't think I could ever have left the cult on my own."

This kind of testimony fuels the zeal of supporters of deprogramming, who insist that there must be some way to rescue cult victims. It also inspires sympathy for parents who believe that their cult-estranged loved ones have lost their minds and must be forcibly removed from the cult "for their own good."

"If we had failed to try to rescue our daughter (through deprogramming) we would have been less than responsible and loving," said the mother of an unsuccessfully deprogrammed Moonie on an NBC documentary of the Unification Church.

Another mother has emphatically said, "We just couldn't stand by and do nothing. We were so afraid that our daughter would never leave the Krishnas and that she would suffer permanent mental and physical damage if she stayed. She was so pale and thin. She had graduated from college with high marks, but after several months in the cult, she seemed so spacy. We felt that she was brainwashed and couldn't leave by herself. We had to rescue her for her own good and because we love her."

Parents who choose deprogramming do so out of genuine concern and usually feel they are choosing the lesser of two evils, but no programming program is foolproof. It offers no guarantees. Parents who choose deprogramming take a calculated risk in alienating their children should the procedure fail. An unsuccessful deprogramming, almost without exception, drives the member further into the cult and further estranges him or her from the family. Some members then sue their parents and deprogrammers for infringement of civil and religious liberties.

"ZOMBIES, ROBOTS, AND DEAD MEN?"

Despite many positive reports, upon careful reflection, there are some serious philosophical questions related to deprogramming.

Philosophically, deprogramming is based on a false premise. It is assumed that the cult member has literally lost control of his or her mind and, therefore, must be rescued.

Consider the assumptions evident in these statements: "It appears to us that many [cult members] do become, for all practical purposes, the robots they are often called." (Conway and Siegelman, cult researchers)

" . . . the members' minds cease to be and they develop a mental condition, [and] become a vegetable . . . their minds [are] destroyed . . . [the cult members] are incapable of thinking or making decisions . . . They [the cults] take a person's mind away from him and make it impossible for him to act on his own." (Ted Patrick)

"You're a zombie, a robot. Your eyes are vacant, your veins are sticking out, your pupils are dilated and your skin is pale . . . You're dead, man!" (Deprogrammer Ford Greene to a Moonie)

"They [cult members] are literally robots." (Former aide to many of the top deprogrammers)

Law professor Richard Delgado, the anticultists' chief legal champion, has argued that the First Amendment does not apply in cult situations because freedom of religion depends on freedom of thought, which a brainwashed cult member cannot possess. (See "Religious Totalism: Gentle and Ungentle Persuasion Under the First Amendment." Southern California Law Review, Vol. 51, No. 1, 1977).

These and many other depictions of cult members as being subhuman or mindless are inaccurate, if not irresponsible. A cult member is a conditioned, misguided, and indoctrinated zealot, but not incapable of thought.

Upon close examination this assumption of total mind

control is implausible and inconsistent. If the thinking of all cult members is impaired, how can some members make the decision—an action that requires thought—to leave? How can some members engage in formal or informal reevaluation—a process that requires reasoning, comparative analysis, and conceptual projection? And most obvious, if they are zombies, how do cult members function in day-to-day living, which requires continuous thought and decision-making—buying food, moving around the city or countryside, and all the other components of daily life?

In the final analysis, the very process of deprogramming disproves the original premise that the member's mind is incapable of functioning. The essential core of deprogramming is an intense form of reevaluation. And the process requires that the individual be capable of reasoning and mental agility. Since the first premise is inaccurate, it logically follows that the concept built upon it—deprogramming—is unsound.

THE BRAINWASHING THEORY

The term "brainwashing" originated in the Chinese communist revolutionary colleges, where individuals were subjected to ideological conversion to Maoism. The Chinese brainwashing or thought reform has much in common with cultic indoctrination processes, including its goals: reshaping a person's perspectives and beliefs and replacing them with the "correct" ideology. The crux of the matter is that, although the thought reform process does alter personalities and beliefs and sometimes drastically, it does not drain the brain of conscious thought nor render its subjects mindless machines.

To quote thought reform expert Dr. Robert J. Lifton: "Behind this web of semantic . . . confusion [concerning the thought reform process] lies an image of 'brainwashing' as an all-powerful, irresistible, unfathomable, and magical method of achieving total control over the human mind. It is of course *none of these things* . . ." [emphasis added by authors].

Berkeley psychologist and student of the cult phenomenon, Dick Anthony, asserts: "Research shows that intellectual and emotional function does not differ significantly between present and former members nor between deprogrammed and voluntary ex-members. This is contrary to what one would expect if descriptions of cult members as brainwashed zombies were accurate."

A VIGILANTE MOVEMENT

Another misgiving about deprogramming is that it is wide open to abuse. Why? Because deprogramming is essentially a cross between a vigilante and a black-market activity.

Deprogramming, which purports to offer aid to the mentally distressed cultist, is not under the auspices or the supervision of mental health authorities. Most deprogrammers are untrained in proper mental health procedures and are not bound by the ethics of the profession.

Some hard-core proponents of deprogramming seem to have difficulty interpreting any cult experience outside of the total brainwashing frame of reference. Some cannot conceive, for example, that a member could simply mature, discard a cultic commitment, and ease back into normal society without the aid of a deprogrammer. And although most deprogrammers may be conscientious and sincere, there are deprogramming charlatans who have fleeced distraught parents of many thousands of dollars.

RECONVERSION?

Some students of the cults see deprogramming as a reconversion. Psychologist Dick Anthony told a Colloquium on Alternative Religions:

Deprogramming those who for one reason or another have not yet left (the cult) voluntarily usually involves converting them from one type of movement to another;

that is, deprogramming is really conversion to the anticult movement. This disguises the member's original motives for joining the group, which usually have something to do with a moral confusion very common in contemporary society . . . The anticult group becomes another group which the member can rely on for simple answers to complex problems. Whereas the cult blamed all the cult's problems on the larger society, the anticult movement blames all the member's problems on the cult.

According to Dr. Anthony, scholarly literature shows that "deprogramming is not helpful therapy." Extremist measures, in whatever form, cannot help an ex-member put the cult experience into a proper perspective.

THE DANGERS OF DEPROGRAMMING

Legally unchecked deprogramming invites interference with non-cultic groups and situations, such as radical political allegiances, fringe religions, and alternate life-styles. If a parent can persuade a deprogrammer that a young person is exhibiting the alleged symptoms of "brainwashing," and is, therefore, under mind control, then the person can become a candidate for deprogramming. These symptoms are stereotypical and so vague as to be license for discrimination and abuse.

Already individuals have been deprogrammed who have had no cult affiliation, but have simply adopted a lifestyle held in disfavor by the middle-of-the-road majority.

Sociologist David G. Bromley reports two such cases:

Ted Patrick was hired by a mother in Oregon to deprogram her 31-year-old daughter who, the mother maintained, was under the psychological influence of her fiancee. *No* religious group or beliefs were involved. The mother simply disapproved of the boyfriend. On another occasion, Patrick was hired by the Greek Orthodox parents of two young women, ages 21 and 23, because the parents were upset that their daughters had resisted the traditional Greek custom of living at home until the parents found them "suitable" husbands.

The Reithmiller trial in Cincinnati, Ohio, in April 1982, involved twenty-year-old Stephanie Reithmiller, whose parents were convinced that she was under the mind control of her allegedly lesbian roommate. The deprogrammers hired by the parents pointed to Stephanie's weight loss, emotional and financial dependency on her roommate, and a separation from her family as evidence of mind control and the subsequent need for deprogramming. This use of the mind control concept knows no bounds and smacks of witch hunting.

Indeed, sociologists Anson Shupe and David Bromley reported in their book *The New Vigilantes: Deprogrammers, Anti-Cultists and the New Religions* that "by the end of the decade there was very little in the area of religious belief or practice that could not be classified as cultic by some anti-cult spokesperson."

It is interesting to note that Pat Robertson, of The Christian Broadcasting Network, has denounced deprogramming and pending legislation favoring deprogramming as a threat against Christians. "The legislation is against the Moonies, but these laws will be turned as weapons against Christians."

ANTICULT LEGISLATION

Is legally checked deprogramming the answer to the problem?

It does not appear to be. Deprogramming itself is based on coercion and the violation of a person's free will, and the law knows no heresy. Who is going to establish the limits and define the terms of exactly what constitutes a "cult?"

Much of the proposed countercult legislation concerns conservatorship, which has been called "legal kidnapping" or "legal deprogramming." This would be an expansion of a law originally designed to protect the elderly who may be senile or mentally unstable. The writ of conservatorship says that a court can appoint a legal guardian for the incompetent adult—usually on short notice and without the person being present at a formal hearing. Such a guardianship can be granted for a thirty-to-sixty-day period. Some parents, claiming their children are incompetent, have used this writ to retrieve them from a cult.

But some courts have put dampers on such legal action. The most well-known court case involving such a use of the conservatorship writ took place in California. A lower court appointed guardians for five young adult members of the Unification Church. A Superior Court ruled: "It was a violation of young adults' rights to religious freedom for court to appoint their parents as their temporary conservators for purposes of 'deprogramming' them of ideals allegedly instilled by religious cult" (Katz vs. Superior Court, 73 Cal. App. 3D, 952, at 234, 1977).

The court required that an individual must be "gravely disabled" before being forcibly removed from a religious group.

As Thomas Robbins, a postdoctoral fellow in the sociology department at Yale University, noted: "In short, it is beyond the authority of the state to employ coercion to maintain each citizen in a state of optimal mental health."

Even a layperson's review of some proposed anticult legislation reveals that they are an invitation, even a demand, for the government to violate the First Amendment: "Congress shall make no law respecting an establishment of religion, or prohibiting the free exercise thereof. . ."

One proposed bill (which never passed) would have declared the promoting of a pseudo-religion a felony. Other efforts have tried to enact legislation that would make it easy for an individual to be forcibly removed from a religious group that is thought to practice brainwashing. As attorney Jon E. LeMoult said, "The next step, of course, would be to outlaw various practices of the religious groups themselves. Consider the possibility of a law which would outlaw brainwashing . . . Would the court be entitled to prohibit the Hare Krishna movement from engaging in ritual chanting? Could pentecostal religious sects be prohibited from speaking in tongues, fundamentalists from memorizing Bible verses? . . . Abandoning legal protections for a particular segment of society whose beliefs are disapproved is a dangerous experiment."

However, this is not to say that religion should protect criminal acts. A 1982 FBI Law Enforcement Bulletin clarified the government's role with respect to crimes committed by religious groups: "Since religious beliefs alone pose no threat to the rights of others, there can be no State interference with these rights. However, when such beliefs are translated into action, the sincerity of those beliefs, whether the activity is harmful to individuals or whether the activity involves fraud or deception, may be scrutinized by the State and limited constitutionally." Cultic, authoritarian religious groups, while they have a right to exist, are certainly not above the law.

A PLEA

However, the opponents of cults should temper their indignation, anger, and hurt with a sensible assessment of the implications and consequences of their proposed legislations and anticult activities. The attitude that something—anything—has to be done and done now to counter the cults can be harmful to all of us in the long run. The anticult movement must guard against the very disease it strives to cure—cultlike fanaticism.

This viewpoint does not mean that I have no empathy for those who have lost loved ones to cults. In addition to losing five years of my life, I also temporarily lost two children to a cult. I know the pain. But I still advocate caution regarding anticult activities.

6.   Postcult Problems

"I know they're out to get me. After all, I know too much about the cult's affairs. . ."

"Man, I've been out [of the cult] for six months and I still haven't found a job. The interviewers just look at me like I'm some kind of freak.

"It's lonely in the world. At least back in the cult, I had some friends."

These are but a few of the complaints voiced by ex-cultists returning to a society which is ill-equipped and unprepared to help them make successful reentry.

There is a pattern to the problems experienced by most ex-cultists. These problems range from a lack of self-confidence to a religious disillusionment to such practical matters as going back to school or finding a job. The average ex-member should expect to encounter some short-term problems, at the very least, and perhaps some more far-reaching ones.

Reported among the most common are: Nightmares of being trapped inside the cult or pursued by angry cult members, unusual phobias, aimlessness, fear of reprisal by the cult, confusion, loneliness, family conflicts, loss of faith, and difficulty in thinking and making decisions. The healing process continues most smoothly when ex-members recognize they are not unique nor alone in their struggles.

CULT-RELATED NIGHTMARES
The traumatic act of leaving a cult may be registered unconsciously and may only later manifest itself. For

example, cult-related nightmares may continue for many months after defection.

Jan C., a bright young woman in her middle twenties, found she was afraid to go to sleep at night because of a recurring nightmare in which members of her former cult were angrily chasing her. She often awakened in a cold sweat after dreaming that she had been forced onto the edge of a cliff by the irate cultists. Jan finally sought professional counseling and her doctor prescribed a mild sedative to help her sleep. About a year later the dreams ceased, and Jan discontinued the medication. Jan feels that, if she had only known that nightmares are a common postcult experience, she might have recovered more quickly.

FEAR OF CULT RETALIATION

Victoria J., an exceptionally pretty, diminutive woman of Italian descent, is now full of enthusiasm and self-confidence. It's hard to imagine that her life was once blighted by the fear that stalks many ex-cultists—the fear of cult retaliation.

As a high-ranking official in one of the Eastern cults, there was some basis for her fear. She possessed extensive knowledge of the cult's questionable financial affairs. Certain unsolved deaths of cult members, ex-members, and critics of the cult fueled her anxiety. She lived in constant dread for nine months, during which time she developed ulcers.

"I tried to think rationally," Victoria said, "but it was difficult, knowing that the members of my cult were capable of anything—even violence in the name of 'God's love.' It helped when I talked with other ex-cultists and found that they were afraid too.

"But it was my grandmother, a very wise woman, who gave me the best advice. She said, 'Victoria, that group is not omniscient or all-powerful, as you think. In time you will be able to put them out of your mind. In the meantime, try concentrating on good thoughts and on building good, solid relationships.'

"I followed her advice and, after a while, I just wasn't afraid anymore. Now, although I acknowledge the power and danger of some of the cults. I am not living in terror that they are coming for me. For four years there has been no attempt at retaliation."

Indeed, most cults don't take the trouble to trace every ex-member. Once a member is no longer bringing in money, it's "out of sight, out of mind."

Ex-members who are actively speaking out against cults should be more cautious, however. The following suggestions might make the threat of cult retaliation less frightening:

- Request an unlisted number from the telephone company.
- Use a post office box for all cult-related correspondence.
- Consider filing suit against the cult. I won a suit for "misrepresentation of ideals" and "alienation of affection" and was awarded the sum of a million and a half dollars. Though the money will likely never be paid, a moral victory was won and the cult was subsequently reluctant to harass me.

There is an old saying that a king has no power over his subjects unless they render him that power. The ex-member must make a conscious effort to reclaim the control the cult once exercised over him or her.

PHILOSOPHICAL QUESTIONS

At one time or another, most of us have questioned the meaning of life, but few of us have had the rug of our basic convictions torn out from under us as violently as have the ex-members of cults. Because their system of belief has so completely betrayed them, ex-members must make deeper philosophical inquiries than the average person is inclined to make. They must try to uncover their own basic assumptions about reality (metaphysics), values (aesthetics), and knowledge—or how we know what we know (epistemology). Identifying these often unconsciously held premises is an essential step in separating the wheat of the sound and rational from the chaff of the cult-inspired, illogical, and misleading.

This will require hard thinking and delving into the writings of the world's great philosophers. Many simple study guides to philosophy are available at public libraries. As ex-members build houses of understanding, they will need bricks made of the wisdom of great thinkers and mortar made of sound reasoning.

RELIGION

Religious problems are treated exclusively in another chapter. It suffices to say here that many ex-members have serious religious misgivings. They have been badly burned, and need time for their faith to be restored. This healing process must not be rushed.

LONELINESS

Loneliness is one of the most common and most painful postcult problems. Ex-members have left behind friends and emotional ties. Many who have spent a number of years in a cult have described themselves as practically friendless when they emerged.

"When I first began to rebuild my life," said Frank K., a former member of the Children of God, "I found that most of my high-school friends had moved away. After all, I had spent five years in the cult and had lost contact with my old friends. . . . I (had) alienated myself from them. It was really difficult to start over."

Frank admits that, in his loneliness, he once thought of returning to the cult, because at least he had some friends there. "But I dropped that idea quickly," he laughed wryly. "In fact, the more I thought of my friends back in the cult, the more I realized we had been like fellow prisoners. We were never allowed to communicate with each other about ourselves or our feelings. We were expected to spend all our time discussing the Bible or the letters of our leader, Moses David. It is impossible to build lasting relationships without communication."

Frank stuck out the lonely periods and has now formed a close circle of friends at college and is seeing a young woman regularly. He eventually came to understand, as do many ex-members, that the warmth he felt from his recruiter was really a manipulative device to entice him and that the "family" relationships within the cult were really empty, mocking shells.

SOCIAL AWKWARDNESS

Sally P., now a successful legal secretary, explained her insecurity and lack of poise following her experience with an Eastern cult:

"When I was with people after leaving the cult, I hadn't the slightest idea what to do or say. We had been indoctrinated with the idea that it was sinful to talk about anything except the cult doctrine. It was unbelievably difficult to make the transition from that austere, cult-imposed silence to making small talk."

However, Sally was able to use the cult-imposed technique of attentive silence to her advantage. She became known as a "good listener." Later she began to interject leading, thoughtful questions into conversations. Her quiet interest in the speaker gained her the self-confidence to move beyond listening and into animated conversations.

"Within the framework of the cult, I was a one-dimensional pawn. I had no thoughts, feelings, or experiences of my own. I've been out of the cult long enough to develop skills in these areas. Conversation comes naturally now."

But such transitions take time.

HEALTH

Because little attention is given to the health of the cult member, a complete medical check-up may be necessary upon leaving.

Many ex-members like Kathy Hansen of Minneapolis complain of burnout. Kathy was a member of the Children of God for six-and-a-half years and lived under the most stressful of conditions.

"My health had seriously deteriorated by the time I left the group," she said. "I had no vitamin reserve at all and, when the excitement of leaving wore off, I suffered a complete physical collapse.

"At one point while I was still with the group, my hair rapidly began to turn gray. When I discovered it was caused by stress, I began to 'demand' more help with my responsibilities, tried to eat better, and took vitamins. I was run-down most of the time, but had to work, sick or well, since sickness was considered merely God's judgment for spiritual weakness. Even though I was often sick, visits to the doctor were rare. The group relies mainly on 'faith healing' for most medical needs."

Illness, infections, and neglected health problems seem all too common among the destructive cults. Many ex-members, like Kathy, suffer postcult medical problems. Those who have escaped actual physical illness are still under the tremendous stress of defecting and the pressures of beginning a new life. Ex-members need to be aware of this and learn how to be kind to themselves. They no longer are under the cult mandate to "save the world." But they must begin to save themselves by giving their bodies an opportunity to recover and by seeking medical advice if necessary.

Cult living forces one into an artificial state of emergency. Body and mind must be retaught to relax. There are many good books on relaxation. Quiet music has also been shown to have a definite soothing effect. Whatever the method, it is imperative that the mind and body, readied for fight or flight during cult days, be returned to a normal state as soon as possible.

MENTAL HEALTH

A minority of ex-members have been so manipulated and damaged by the cults that their mental health is impaired. In the words of Dr. John Clark, Jr., "They are simply not able to use their minds as tools of survival and are supremely difficult to treat."

Though most ex-members are not in such a serious condition, concern about mental health is warranted and treatment should be sought if needed.

SUBJUGATION OF WOMEN

Within most cults, women are generally viewed as incapable, subservient beings, often the targets of scorn and ridicule.

In the Krishna holy book *Bhagavad-Gita,* women are described as "very prone to degradation . . . generally not very intelligent, and therefore, not trustworthy." In one of the Bible-based cults, women are instructed to walk behind the men, fingering dirt in their pockets to remind themselves of their inferior position. The Children of God blatantly exploit women through religious prostitution and the condoning of rape.

In such an environment, a female may lose pride in her femininity and her self-confidence may ebb away; men may learn to scorn women and suppress the innate feminine side of their own personalities.

An ex-member needs to critically reevaluate all the information he or she received in the group pertaining to sexuality and sex-related roles. Left unexamined, much of this programming can linger on to cause problems with opposite-sex relationships. This mysogyny needs to be uprooted and replaced with positive attitudes—women liking and taking pride in themselves, and men liking and respecting women.

A BAD EXPERIENCE WITH COERCIVE DEPROGRAMMING

If an ex-cult member's deprogramming experience was particularly painful, he or she may use it as an excuse to return to the cult. But such thinking is illogical. A deprogrammer's "wrongs" do not make a cult "right." Such thinking is as absolutist as that on which the cults thrive, and ignores the many shades of gray in a world which is never clearly black or white.

"My deprogramming was just awful," recalls Joan. "My deprogrammer picked on me, was ignorant, and shouted all the time. He even made a pass at me, and I resented him for that. The people working with him weren't much better—real party-lovers, staying up all hours of the night, drinking and smoking. I found that hard to take after my years in a puritanical cult.

"Nevertheless, I feel my deprogrammer saved my life in bringing me out of the cult. I mean that quite literally in light of what happened at Jonestown. I believe something like that could happen in any cult. While I almost hated my deprogrammer at times, I am grateful for what he did for me.

"I guess after a while I came to realize that deprogrammers are human, just like the rest of us. They're not pedestal material. They are just ordinary people doing a job, despite their sometimes glaring failures."

UNEMPLOYMENT

Unemployment is among the most frequently cited of the postcult problems. Many cults recruit high-school students who are easy, impressionable prey. A teenaged convert may emerge from a cult in his or her early twenties with no marketable skills. Many other converts forsake their careers or advanced schooling to join a cult, and find it extremely difficult to take up where they left off.

Other reasons for unemployment among ex-members are more personal: lack of motivation, confusion about goals or direction in life, or even a cult-inspired fear or contempt of a secular job.

Ex-members often express anger when they realize what they have lost to a cult. Many use this anger to fuel a speedy return to the mainstream. Some enter college or apply for vocational training through government or vocational rehabilitation funding. A school situation seems to ease the transition into the world of employment.

"I simply refused to be a victim," claims George C., ex-member of the Unification Church. "Moon ruined the three years of my life I spent with his group. Those years are lost and can't be reclaimed, I couldn't let him ruin any more of my life.

"I've had to work harder than my peers to establish myself professionally because of those wasted years . . . but I was determined to make it."

The drive to overcome the past is essential to combatting postcult unemployment. The lives of many ex-members testify to the fact that successful employment *can* be found after leaving a cult.

LACK OF SELF-CONFIDENCE

A major postcult problem underlying many of the others is a lack of self-confidence. Destructive cults systematically erode self-esteem, the first step toward the annihilation of self and the mastery of an individual. Cult members are taught to devalue themselves and scorn God's highest creation—humanity.

"My years in the cult conditioned me to feel inadequate," says George. "This belief was initially instilled by the leaders through their doctrines and teachings and was systematically reinforced—often in front of a roomful of people. Then there were the public 'confession sessions.'

We were further humiliated in other ways, such as being instructed to beg for food or root through garbage for discarded goods behind grocery stores. After I left, it took me quite a while to learn to respect myself again.

"Though the cults resort to this method of controlling their members, I find nothing in the Bible that says we are to hate ourselves. On the contrary, it tells us that we are created in the image of God, and that we are to love our neighbors *as we love ourselves!* It was quite a revelation when I rediscovered those teachings!"

Self-confidence comes from believing oneself to be capable and competent—a worthy person. After George accepted the fact that the cult had programmed him to hate himself, he began to use positive thinking to replace those self-defeating thoughts. Other helpful antidotes include: cultivating emotionally supporting relationships and improving one's physical appearance and surroundings.

DEPRESSION

"Depression overcomes us when we lose ourselves," says psychologist Max Parks of Akron, Ohio. Often a postcultic depression dissipates and eventually disappears as the ex-member reclaims a sense of self, rebuilds a life, identifies his or her abilities and interests, makes friends, and takes an interest in the world.

It is important, however, that an ex-member recognize the roots of depression and take charge of his or her own life, rather than abdicating the responsibility to another.

If postcultic depression becomes severe, one must seek professional help. Seeking such help is the responsible, not the "weak," course of action.

DISILLUSIONMENT

Of all the negative effects experienced by an ex-cultist, one of the most cruelly debilitating is disillusionment with life and the loss of ideals. The cults appeal to the highest and most heroic aspect of humanity—idealism. Then the cult commits the ultimate exploitation—using that idealism to enslave young men and women.

When this hard reality confronts ex-members, when beliefs have apparently betrayed them, everything may seem worthless and futile. Ideals and convictions often seem naive, even treacherous. It seems nothing is worth personal dedication. This understandable cynicism will, with proper assistance, moderate in time.

Philip P., an ex-cultist who is currently studying philosophy at an Eastern university, recalls suffering from disillusionment. "I felt I could never get excited about living again," he muses. "I felt apathetic, drained of enthusiasm. In talking with another ex-member about my feelings, I discovered this to be a common reaction. I guess it's like a loss of innocence. I came to understand how the cult had manipulated my idealism and exploited it for their own use, but it has caused me to be more realistic about what I want and expect in life. I do have ideals, but I will be careful never to let anyone exploit them again."

One has the feeling that Philip's sensitivities have been dealt a harsh blow and that it will be some time before he can truly feel that it is safe to trust again.

GOAL-SETTING

Setting goals is vitally important for the ex-member. Without them he will feel aimless and ineffectual, and the job of getting on with life will seem overwhelming. A road map is needed.

An ex-member needs to plan some short-term, median, and long-term goals. A short-term goal consists of what one hopes to accomplish in the next few days; the median goal, plans for the next six months, and long-term goals establish hope for the rest of one's life. The latter are the most awesome and may require the member to do some dreaming.

Ex-members should let their minds wander, considering all the possibilities, not ruling out anything: "What could I do if there were no obstacles? What could I do if there were no one else to consider?"

From the answers to these and other questions, he or she should be able to hone some realistic goals. Career counseling, which includes interest and aptitude tests, can be helpful and may be in order.

ADAPTING TO DAILY LIVING

Ex-members emerging from a highly structured environment, where all decisions were dictated, often find themselves unable to manage time effectively. To save themselves from a quagmire of wasted time, ex-members need the self-discipline of a daily schedule. They need to take charge of their lives and direct them according to personally chosen schedules. After being completely dependent upon the motivation and direction of the cult, this schedule making and keeping is a difficult, but necessary, task.

Carol D., an ex-Divine Light Mission member, believes the best procedure involves organizing small parts of one's day, and, only when that is mastered, moving on to more comprehensive organizing and scheduling of days, weeks, and years.

FINANCIAL PROBLEMS

Ex-members are often in a vulnerable financial position— either having no money at all or being too inexperienced to handle it properly. As a rule, an ex-member walks away from a cult empty-handed.

Parents of babies and small children who have left their mates in the cult, may have no alternative for support except from their own parents or from welfare. The bitter taste in the mouth left from such hardship is not easily forgotten, but can be used as motivation toward self-sufficiency. An ex-member in such a situation should be careful to avoid becoming lazy or discouraged and tarrying in this stage longer than necessary.

Steven Blake of Minneapolis, an ex-member of the

Children of God, provides additional insight: "A person who has been deprived of material things may be tempted to spend money foolishly when he first gets a job." Inexperience and lack of budgeting skills and self-restraint are at the heart of postcult financial difficulties. But these skills can be learned and applied.

Sometimes an ex-member has philosophical problems with the idea of money and possessions. Most cults teach that money is evil and immoral. The ex-member must relearn the definition of money—the tangible evidence of work and effort. It is a tool, a practical means of exchange for needed goods and services, in itself, neither evil nor immoral. A worker has a right to the money received in exchange for time and labor.

DESTRUCTIVE DEPENDENCIES

It is almost impossible for anyone who has not "been there" to comprehend the tremendous loss suffered by ex-cultists who have left behind them a package-deal life, full of love, support, and absolute answers—all structured around a purpose and goals. In its place sits a gaping void. Within the cult, the member was allegedly one of God's elite, one of His chosen few. This gave the member an exalted sense of superiority. When the member leaves and becomes "just another person," he or she may feel quite a letdown. Some ex-members, unable to adjust to their emotional losses, attempt to fill the void with other, sometimes destructive, dependencies, such as excessive alcohol or drug use or becoming "hooked" on a particular person.

One can start to combat such destructive dependencies by recognizing them for what they are—miserable substitutes for wholeness that divert people from facing their lack of meaning, purpose, and motivation. Ex-members must acknowledge the loss of their dream, mourn for it, and then move on to discover what really is most important in their lives. They may find a clue when they analyze the reasons why they committed themselves to the cult in the first place. If an ex-member explores his or her inner self and truly seeks truth, he or she may be surprised to find that the kingdom of God is within—not without.

PERSONAL RELATIONSHIPS

Many ex-cultists experience problems relating to members of the opposite sex, stemming from strong cultic influence in the area of sexuality. Except for a few cults that mandate or promote promiscuity, most cults are fanatically strict when it comes to relationships between the sexes, and exercise authority over even the most intimate aspects of the lives of their members. Most encourage celibacy or near-celibacy. After being in the Unification Church three years, a couple is "matched" or engaged by Rev. Moon. Then they must wait another three years before consummating the marriage. This practice was confirmed when Rev. Moon was forced to testify under oath in a May, 1982 court case. Married couples in the Krishna movement are only allowed to have intercourse once a month—when the woman is most fertile. In this same cult small children are made to take cold showers to "stem their desires."

An ex-member of a cult that suppresses sexual expression might find it extremely difficult to relate to persons of the opposite sex, finding even an innocent date terrifying. An ex-member of a promiscuous group might be wary of the opposite sex, afraid of being exploited again or thought of as shameful for the behavior enforced by the cult."

"I'm afraid of men now," confesses one ex-member of the Children of God. "I feel as though they can see right through me and know what I've done. I don't know if I can ever trust a man again, or if there is a man out there worthy of my trust." This woman was in her late twenties when she left her husband and joined the cult, where she was forced into religious prostitution. Through deprogramming she left after only six months, but her husband, with whom she desired reconciliation, could not live with the knowledge of what she had done and divorced her. Now, a year later, through sound professional counseling and supportive friends, this woman is recovering from her fear of exploitation.

Ex-members returning from either extreme to society need to restore a balance to their lives and relationships. Professional counseling may be required if the ability for normal heterosexual interaction has been severely damaged. In less severe cases, a sharply critical examination of the cult's attitude toward sexuality may be sufficient to restore this balance.

Sometimes out of despair or acute loneliness, an ex-member will enter into an unwise marriage or serious relationship. One psychiatrist interviewed recommended no intense romantic relationships for eighteen months to two years after leaving a cult. He warned that one should come to a serious relationship like marriage as a whole person with something to give, not as a beggar with only desperate needs to be filled.

A recent ex-member contemplating a permanent commitment should carefully evaluate his reasons and motives. Is he using this relationship to compensate for some feelings of inadequacy or need? If so, then the marriage may become an even bigger problem. It would be wise to defer the commitment.

FAMILY CONFLICTS

If family problems existed before the cult experience, they probably will not disappear when a member comes home. The expectation that the return will, in itself, resolve family problems is unrealistic and could prove harmful if it prevents the tackling of the original problems.

In Jean C.'s case, problems in her family were the catalyst that drove her into the cult. "I didn't feel loved or wanted by my parents," she explains. "We couldn't communicate. I felt ignored. I was a young teenager who didn't understand her parents or herself. The cult seemed more caring and more powerful than my parents, so I ran to it for refuge."

Jean's problems with her overly reserved parents persisted long after she left the cult. A family counselor wisely advised her to initiate communication with her parents. "It wasn't easy," Jean admits. "We had never really talked about anything before, not even my reasons for wanting to join the cult. It seemed that they preferred to pretend it had never happened. I took the first step and opened up about my thoughts and feelings. It was tough going at first, but in time we got to the point where we could communicate."

Some ex-members have a strong desire to escape their excessively concerned family. Paddy H. was deprogrammed from the Krishnas two years ago. "My parents were very involved with my whole deprogramming. After it was over I desperately needed to get away from them. I felt suffocated. My stay at a rehabilitation center gave me the break from them that I needed. I get along fine with them now."

Not all family problems are resolved as easily as were Jean's or Paddy's. If the problems are serious and persistent, some parents are unwilling to seek needed counsel because they perceive this as a second failure—the first being their child's cult experience. These parents need to recognize the cult involvement as a cry for help. Ignoring that cry could be disastrous for all concerned.

Upon emerging into society, the ex-member often needs *intense* parental support while healing from the trauma of the past few months or years. When ready to stand alone, he or she will once more wish to break away and become an independent entity. This step is healthy and should be encouraged. Parents can assist in the emancipation of the young person by applauding any attempts at finding independence.

THE JOURNEY BACK

I left the Children of God in 1977, after five years of membership. As I sailed from the cult center in Norway, bound for my parents' home in England, I was not fully aware of the long and difficult journey that lay beyond the completion of that voyage. After reaching England, I still faced the arduous trip back to the real world and to the real, integral self.

From my present vantage point some years later, I am able to appreciate the difficulty of that mental journey, and the vital importance of the support of friends and unflinching honesty with myself. These are perhaps the most important factors in arriving safely at the destination.

These and other problems that beset the ex-member are often difficult and trying. However, working through them builds character. Of course, there are easier ways to gain personal strength, determination, and independence than to go through a cult experience, but the ex-member should take advantage of the opportunity to overcome obstacles and become a survivor.

7. Getting Help, Finding Support

"Leaving the cult was a shattering experience," confided one ex-member. "I had nothing—no faith, no money, no job . . . I had to rebuild my life from scratch."

One is reminded of these lines from Rudyard Kipling's poem "If":

> [If you can] watch the things you gave your life to, broken
> And stoop and build 'em with worn-out tools. . .
> Yours is the Earth and everything that's in it.
> And—which is more—you'll be a man, my Son!

Upon reentering the real world, the former cult member must relearn how to think and reason. His or her delicate self, emerging from a fantasy world of a cult leader, needs a supportive milieu. This can be provided through organized rehabilitation alternatives, professional help, or even through strong supportive relationships.

This period of postcult readjustment or rehabilitation, during which the ex-member must restructure a shattered life, mourn for a broken dream, and get on with the business of living, can be difficult. However, help is available.

TAKING RESPONSIBILITY

The members who simply walk away from their groups have a need to put their cult experience into perspective and integrate it into the rest of their lives. The tendency, which unfortunately is promoted by the deprogramming rationale, is to place the responsibility for cult involvement on the group and its "brainwashing" techniques, ignoring any personal problems, contemporary moral confusion, or other factors which may have predisposed the individual to cult membership.

Personal crises are often accompanied by an immature refusal to accept responsibility. Someone or something else is always to blame. However, this need to absolve guilt through denial of responsibility should be viewed as part of a transitional phase rather than a permanent interpretation of the cult experience.

These thoughts were perceptively presented by psychologist Dick Anthony at the Colloquium on Alternative Religion:

> Rather than acknowledge that they were temporarily quite willing to surrender freedom of thought, some ex-members may prefer to externalize responsibility for prior commitments and affirm that they were brainwashed . . . I would not absolve individuals of responsibility for their membership in these movements. Individuals should understand where their vulnerability comes from, take responsibility for it, and achieve over a period of time a mature and responsible resolution of their original problems . . . rather than scapegoating cults. . . . Unless members and ex-members understand the reasons for their vulnerability, they will continue to have difficulty developing the strength necessary to deal with a morally problematic secular society. That is why I advocate a [voluntary] counseling approach . . . we must help these individuals with their personal problems. To do otherwise is to ignore the true nature of the situation.

It takes time and effort for an ex-member to come to the point where he or she can see the cult experience in perspective and take some responsibility, but denying that responsibility can ultimately retard one's psychological maturity.

"You just can't cut x number of years out of your life by

saying 'That wasn't the real me during that time, because my mind was being controlled.' You must own your experience," observed an ex-member.

CONFUSION

"Floating" is a term coined in the countercult world to describe periods of vacillation experienced by many ex-members early in rehabilitation. It is a confused state of mind—a state of emotional limbo—in which the ex-member feels uncertainty about his defection, and may feel that he is caught between two lives.

Martin O. described his periods of floating:

After my deprogramming, I sometimes went through short periods of intense uncertainty. One minute I was positive that I was doing the right thing in leaving the cult; then I wasn't sure any more. I seemed to slip back into the cult state of mind and back into their programming.

I was under their control again. It was unnerving and confusing. I would speak in a childish voice, my pupils would become dilated and I would begin defending the cult. My rehabilitator and I would sit down and talk about my feelings, doubts, and questions, and then about the inconsistencies and realities of the cult. Then I'd come out of it and touch base with reality again. This floating, which could be triggered by phrases or music or even Bible passages that had been used by the cult, went on for about a month, until I was firmly out and on my feet again.

Leaving a cult is like awakening from a deep sleep and gradually regaining consciousness. During the semi-consciouslike stage, when ex-members are struggling to find themselves again, they can lose their footing, float, and even return to the cult. Ex-members and those around them should be aware of the danger of floating and be ready to meet it with reason, information, steadfastness, and the help and support of other concerned individuals. "Actions stem from the unconscious mind," counsels psychologist Max Parks, echoing a psychiatric tradition of thought. Dr. Parks also views cult involvement as a symptom of underlying problems that need to be resolved. Ex-members may need professional help in understanding their vulnerabilities as well as integrating their experience. Let's look at the various avenues of help available.

REHABILITATION CENTERS

Rehabilitation centers are resocializing units usually run by ex-members. Ideally the centers are sanctuaries from the harassment many defectors receive from their cults. They provide needed services for new ex-members: a strong supportive atmosphere where they can learn to function independently again; education about the mind-manipulative techniques used by the destructive cults; information and facts about the individual cults previously hidden from ex-members; and a safe, semi-sheltered environment where they can ease back into normal living—making decisions, and resuming control of their own lives.

Steve Kemperman wrote favorably of his experience at a rehabilitation center in his book *Lord of the Second Advent*:

> The program was designed as a four-week period where ex-cult members voluntarily could examine their respective religious cult from a point of view outside the group, free from its pressures and influences. It was a time of readjustment to the outside world [during which measures of restraint such as blocked windows and night guards were employed] . . . to keep the cults out . . . [and] to restrain ex-cult members who, being initially confused and psychologically weak, are prone to floating and sudden impulses to return to the cult. . . . Dr. Swope [the Baptist minister who ran the center] explained that

the rehabilitation program practiced restraint, not incarceration.

However, these centers can have their bad, as well as good, points. Andrew Wilson, an unsuccessfully deprogrammed Moonie, has a more negative view of rehabilitation: "Everywhere I went, I was guarded by one or more people. In the house they had chimes set up to warn them if I should decide to make a break for it." These types of restraint are of greatest concern to civil libertarians.

But many ex-members testify that they have been helped by a stay at a rehabilitation center. Ex-members can certainly be of some help to another ex-member who is readjusting to life outside the cult in the same way an alcoholic or former drug user can assist another addict.

Sandy is an ex-member of the Divine Light Mission. She operated a moderately successful rehabilitation center in the Midwest for nine months. Sandy's background in social work makes her one of the few rehabilitators with professional training. Although she has asked that her real name not be disclosed in this book, she provided us with many details about life within a center.

After her own rehabilitation, Sandy came back to her hometown to set up a center staffed by several other ex-members who were experienced in deprogramming and rehabilitation. Funded by advance payments from a group of concerned parents, she rented a house large enough to accommodate the four staff members and four new ex-cultists. Parents belonging to the local chapter of the Individual Freedom Foundation anticult group donated furniture and household equipment to the center.

Sandy's background in social work and her philosophy of moderation help her maintain professional and ethical values within her center.

"We help these people achieve a balance," she says. "We counsel the person to learn how to recognize addictive tendencies and then encourage the development of self-esteem so that such addictions are not necessary. We urge people to think about the reasons for their excesses, instead of just compulsively carrying them out.

"We do not want to force our own personal beliefs on the person coming out of the cult," Sandy explained. "We do help them discover who they are and what their own beliefs are."

The average stay at Sandy's center is one month—at a cost she was reluctant to disclose. During this time ex-members are encouraged to make their own decisions and engage in recreational activities.

The daily activities at the center include one- to three-hour educational sessions that serve as springboards for discussion and interaction. Sandy stresses that these meetings are not encounter therapy sessions since no staff member is professionally qualified to lead such sessions. The material studied centers around theories of mind control, behavior modification techniques, and factual information about the various cults, and includes the writings of Dr. Robert J. Lifton, Dr. Margaret Thaler Singer, Flo Conway, and Jim Siegelman. (See Bibliography for listings of cult-related writings.)

FIGHTING FIRE WITH FIRE

Some deprogrammers and rehabilitators even incorporated as a church in order to enjoy the protection offered religions by the First Amendment. Attorney Paul Traub, who has represented deprogrammers in several court cases, explained:

> The rights and privileges accorded these groups [the cults] gave me an idea . . . If I were to describe the people that I represent [deprogrammers and rehabilitators] as a religious group, I could obtain for my clients the same protection that these cult groups are seeking for themselves. If we called ourselves "agnostic missionaries" and the activities of deprogrammers religious activi-

ties, and said that the deprogrammers are, in fact, religious counselors, their activities would be protected and the perjorative connotations erased.

This idea became a reality for a short period in Ohio, where a rehabilitation center incorporated as "The Church of Job." One of the founders, a deprogrammer, maintained that the church was "based on freeing children from the bondage of false prophets and promoting the Word of God." He also admitted that they were "playing the same game as the cults. We're fighting fire with fire and it comes down to who has the biggest matches."

EVALUATING REHABILITATION CENTERS

Psychologist Trudy Solomon, who has surveyed over one hundred ex-Moonies, found that ex-members who had contact with deprogrammers and rehabilitators had a more negative concept of their cult experience than those ex-members who had no such contact. She also found that "though many [ex-members] felt rehabilitation was unnecessary, few saw it as inherently harmful."

In fact, descriptions of the process sounded more like a summer vacation than anything "therapeutic," and they seemed to give ex-members merely some 'space' between their exits and their entrances back into mainstream society. In many ways, rehabilitation was depicted as being analogous to a halfway house situation. Those who did express negative reactions to rehabilitation either criticized its "anticult" bias or its "exploitation" and its use of newly deprogrammed members undergoing rehabilitation to deprogram others. Most simply saw it as a time to readjust to living in the real world once again.

Two ex-members who participated in the Solomon study candidly described their feelings toward deprogramming and rehabilitation:

"I felt a compulsion from deprogrammers, family, and friends to categorize the Moon experience as negative, even if unconsciously. I resented this and it made it more difficult to find a balance in my post-Moon thinking."

"I was in a miniature anti-Moon, anticult cult. I hardly heard anything else but news about groups."

From a different orientation, Mrs. B., active in rehabilitation for many years, views rehabilitation and its attendant negative concept of the cult experience as imperative for the returning ex-member.

"Deprogramming and rehabilitation are the only ways to leave a cult and not have problems later. These self-help books about how to leave a cult are stupid. It's also stupid for parents to try [to retrieve their child] because the parents don't usually know enough about mind control. They are too emotionally involved and have no patience or understanding [of the experience]. It's easier for the ex-member to open up to a deprogrammer."

The main flaw of the rehabilitation centers is their narrow base of reference—the deprogramming ideology. Some anticult zealots, assuming to help a new ex-member, will insist that he or she interpret the cult experience only within the framework of anti-cult ideology. Ex-members can be suspiciously viewed as being "not quite recovered" if their views are not staunchly anticult. Extremism, intolerance, and close-mindedness cannot help ex-members put their experience into perspective.

PROFESSIONAL COUNSELING

Many ex-members can benefit from professional counseling to help readjust to life outside the cult, understand the cult experience and resolve preexisting problems which may have prompted him or her to join the cult. Some ex-members have been helped immensely by even one session with a mental health professional who is knowledgeable about cults, while others have needed more extensive therapy. Ex-members and those around them should be alert to signs that professional help may be needed.

These signs could include a complete and lasting inability to cope with life, the failure over a period of time to "bounce back" from the cult experience, dependencies on things or other people to give the ex-member's life meaning and purpose, continuous depression, or suicidal tendencies. These and other warning lights signal the need for professional help, and should not be ignored.

Trained psychiatric help may be difficult to find. Take the case of Harry S., who had been out of his Bible-based cult for four years when a frightening experience caused him to question his sanity.

"I hadn't heard from them [the cult leaders] in years," Harry explained, "when out of the blue they contacted me and sent me some of their written material. Reading those writings activated the old cult programming and set up a chain reaction in my brain. Thoughts and feelings that had been dormant suddenly sprang to life. In an ecstatic state, I thought God was speaking to me, telling me to go back to the cult. A thousand Scriptures to rationalize this fact raced through my mind. I couldn't stop the crazy thoughts whirling through my head. It scared me because I wondered if my actions might become as uncontrollable as my thoughts. Finally I thought I heard the words *Go upstairs and choke your children*. It was at that point that I told my wife I needed psychiatric help."

When Harry sought professional help, he found a listening ear, but an absence of knowledge about cults. "The guy wasn't able to explain what had happened to me," Harry said. Harry is still looking for a professional who can understand his problem in relation to his cult experience.

Overloaded with the pressing issues of drug abuse, alcoholism, and disturbances and pathologies of every description, these professionals have tended to ignore the comparatively small, but proliferating, group of ex-cultists who may hesitantly reach out for assistance. Unfortunately, many of the professionals see only the occasional extreme case of suicide or psychosis, discounting the thousands who experience less severe disorders.

Ex-members are not necessarily mentally ill because they were a part of a bizarre cult. If they display symptoms of neurosis or even psychosis, it *may* be due, in part, to long-term trauma induced by cult living. But the well-trained, concerned professional will probe beneath obvious, superficial patterns to uproot underlying causes that may have existed before cult indoctrination. Often ex-cultists are only temporarily emotionally unbalanced. But they *are* in psychic pain, and the helping professionals are in the business of alleviating pain, whatever its source.

Almost every community has a mental health clinic and family service center. If the general counseling available from these agencies does not relieve the ex-cultist's (or the family's) pain, then the parties involved may seek the more extensive counseling of a professional psychologist. The next step would be to secure the services of a psychiatrist, a medical doctor qualified to prescribe medications when necessary.

Of course, your own pastor may be a trained counselor or may be able to refer you to such a person. Unfortunately, the cult ignorance found in the mental health profession is often found in the church office, but this lack of information and sensitivity is slowly dissolving.

A therapist should have some knowledge of cults based on objective scholarship. One clearing house for such scholarship is The Center for the Study of New Religions of the Graduate Theological Union in Berkeley, California. This center has also been active in coordinating an interdisciplinary network of scholars of the cult phenomenon.

THE CENTER ON DESTRUCTIVE CULTISM

The ill effects of the total cult experience are becoming increasingly clear to at least some members of the helping professions. Foremost in the exploration and development of significant new methods of coping with the negative results of cultism is John G. Clark, M. D.

Under the aegis of the American Family Foundation, Dr. Clark and his colleagues, Dr. Michael D. Langone, Dr. Robert E. Schecter, and the Reverend Roger C. B. Daly have founded the Center on Destructive Cultism, located in Boston, Massachusetts. Its purpose is to provide a national focus for theoretical research, the development of professional counselors, and preventive public education.

As a psychiatrist, Dr. Clark uses the therapeutic approach to cult problems. However, he declares that he does not defend only traditional psychiatric approaches to human problems or attack religion or religious beliefs. His hope is that he may help solve and perhaps prevent the developmental problems caused young people by destructive cults. The center is said to be a response to the problems caused individuals, families, and society at large by persons and groups that employ mind-control technologies and irresponsible forms of behavior modification.

THE VALUE OF FRIENDSHIP

Friendship is one of the key elements to a successful rehabilitation. It eases the ex-member's transition back to a world he or she has been taught to hate. It enhances one's self-esteem. It soothes the pain of leaving behind a part of one's life, hopes, and dreams. Often this type of supportive friendship is extended to the new ex-member by other ex-members or by loyal friendship from precult days.

Sarah G. places great value on the support she received during her postcult transition period. "I walked out of my cult after four years. Two very special friends helped me at that time. One was an old high-school buddy who had read a lot about cults and really tried to understand what I was going through. She didn't chide me for joining a cult. Instead she resumed our friendship where we had left off. The other friend was an ex-member whom I met through the local anticult group. There was a special bond of understanding between us because of the common cult experience in our lives.

"During that terrible initial period of readjustment, both friends extended their support to me. I suppose, in a way, they carried me in their arms across the darkest parts of my rehabilitation. They helped me to educate myself about the cult experience. They believed in me when I had no faith in myself. They cared about me and loved me."

Because of the cults' insistence that there is no love outside their particular group, genuine caring can be a most effective antidote to cult involvement.

8. The Church Can Help Heal

An open-minded reading of the Gospel of Mark makes one thing quite clear: Jesus was a Healer. People flocked to Him from far and near, seeking help with their problems, illnesses, and afflictions. Sometimes He was almost crushed in the crowds of those who had heard of His healing powers and had come for relief. First in Galilee, then into Samaria and Judea, word traveled that this carpenter from Nazareth, this man called Jesus, could restore people to spiritual, mental, emotional, and physical health.

Throughout Christian history, healing, health, and a joyous life have been associated with faith in Jesus Christ. Not all of these healings have been accomplished instantaneously. Many healings take place over a period of time and with the help of trained physicians, nurses, counselors, and loved ones. Yet the healings continue.

THE MINISTRY OF HEALING

The church, the body of Christ, the community of those called by the gospel to faith in Christ, was meant to be a healing fellowship. This does not mean that every worship service needs to include prayer over the sick, or an anointing with oil. The healing of Jesus Christ is, first of all, a healing from sin. He mediates our salvation with our heavenly Father and reunites us with God as adopted sons and daughters. All true healing is based on this reconciliation of the shattered parts of our personalities and on reunion with God and our brothers and sisters in Christ.

Physical, mental, and emotional healing can and often does follow from this basic healing of the disease of sin.

Yet the church we know is only "ideally" the healing fellowship. Something in us, in our sinfulness and lack of faith, often keeps us from letting our congregations become "hospitals for sinners." The church that understands itself and its mission as healing, reconciling fellowship will be an ideal place for the victims of cultic misadventure. If we are committed to the healing of broken relationships and to the aiding of the abused, distressed, depressed, and confused, we shall, indeed, fulfill the calling of the church.

THROUGH A GLASS DARKLY

No one can genuinely conceive of God as Friend if he or she does not have a friend on earth! Though we must continue stressing the healing of the broken relationship between humanity and God, honesty and realism cause us to conclude that this healing (salvation) may be possible for the cynical and the abused only after they experience human love, the healing of interpersonal relationships.

We see through a glass darkly, dimly. We understand the heavenly only by the analogies we draw from the earthly. As long as God is seen or defined in reference to the cult leader, we cannot expect the ex-cultist to have faith—in the New Testament sense of trusting in God. Therefore, to be true to the primary mission of saving sinners, we must emphasize healing broken human relationships and up-building the self-image of the ex-member.

PATIENCE

Pastors, parents, friends, and church members may feel a bit bewildered by the attitude of the former cultist toward the church and religious matters. Since his or her sensitive spiritual nature has suffered abuse in the name of God and religion, the ex-cultist is understandably wary of those "selling" religion. The former cult member knows only too well that "everybody talking about heaven ain't going there," and must be forgiven when suspicious of the biblical and theological words that have been misused by cult recruiters and leaders.

Think of the former cultist as you would view the soldier who has been traumatized by combat or imprisonment. There are many striking similarities between the former serviceman brutalized in Korea or Vietnam, and the ex-cultist who has escaped from a destructive cult. Not only have both persons suffered from lack of medical care and good food, from loss of sleep and frequent moves at the whim of leaders who could not be questioned, but they may have had their ideals and beliefs strained or even destroyed by the misdirection of their loyalty and devotion. The ex-soldier may feel abandoned by his country— that his patriotism has been misplaced by the nature of the uncertain conflict in which he was engaged.

If the ex-soldier's hurts and cynicism are directed toward the government or the general idea of patriotism, then it follows that the ex-cultist's hurts and cynicism are undoubtedly directed toward the church and religion in general. Understanding of this possible psychological reaction on the part of the ex-cultist will cause the wise Christian to refrain from encouraging active church involvement too soon.

WINNING THE EX-CULTIST'S TRUST

There's an old saying, "Once bitten, twice shy." How true this is for ex-cultists. Those who feel that religion has been abusive are likely to avoid anything or anyone representative of the church. The ex-cultist must be approached as one would approach anyone who feels hostile toward the church.

Winning the trust of the ex-cultist may not be easy, not only for religious reasons, but because of his or her difficulty in relating to anyone at this time. In the case of groups such as the Hare Krishna, which "retires" its members from the world for a period of time, ex-members may not be ready for interpersonal relations. A young person who has been abused physically, mentally, or sexually by a cult may have deep suspicion of anyone who expresses a personal interest.

Friendship grows out of little acts of kindness and occasional comforting words or bits of helpful advice.

To be a friend to an ex-cultist, one must:

• Be willing to devote whatever time and energy is needed to prove one's friendship.

• Allow the ex-cultist to open up at his or her own pace, avoid being judgmental, and convey sympathy without excess sentimentality.

• Listen receptively without trying to analyze or criticize. The ex-member needs freedom to "dump" a lot of painful material.

Jesus knew how to be a friend. He began a relationship where the person *was*. Prostitute, publican, sinner—were met by Him at the point of their most painful need. Jesus had no words of condemnation for them. He did not measure them by the lofty standards of His own life, only to find them lacking. He spoke to them in words and concepts they could understand. He called them by name. He knew them as only an intimate friend can know another. Then, step by step, He pointed to a better way, a richer, fuller life than they had ever dreamed possible: "I have come that they may have life, and have it to the full" (John 10:10).

REDEEMING RELIGIOUS LANGUAGE

The ex-cultist's story is his or her pain. Listen carefully. Try to clarify in your own mind the nature of the damaging cult. Especially note the religious practices, terms, slogans, symbols, and language used by the cult. These terms and symbols will likely have very different connotations from those used by your church.

For example, the Scripture verse, "Love one another" is interpreted by one cult to mean, "Be prepared to use sexual allure to the point of actual sexual relations in order to draw a prospective recruit into the cult or to extract money from him or her."

It is important to learn this cultic language, in order to correct the misuse of terminology and concepts when the ex-cultist is ready. On the surface, the cult uses the same language spoken in an Evangelical church, but beware of their blatant perversion of meanings.

In addition, careful consideration must be given to the phrasing used when an ex-cultist is invited to become part of a Christian fellowship. Making the mistake of using terms commonly accepted as "Christian" but which have been twisted by the cult might turn such a person away from the church and back to the group.

The ex-cult member is probably carrying a load of guilt and may even be concerned about having left the cult. The ex-member may feel a compulsion to return to the cult to "purge" his or her "sin" in order to reduce personal fear and anxiety, thus using religious terms that are loaded with cultic overtones is extremely dangerous.

CULTIC OVERTONE

Examples of the "cultic overtones" of Christian actions and language are quite easy to cite. Persons involved in the Children of God or The Way, International, who have practiced glossolalia or "speaking in tongues" have reported their uneasiness when attending charismatic services in which members of the church were engaged in this activity. The ex-cultists never returned to those churches because it seemed to them (no matter how fairly or unfairly) that the practices of the charismatics were no different from those of the cult. Perhaps more to the point was the fear aroused within the ex-cultists that they would be irresistibly drawn back into the cult through tongues-speaking.

Even nonreligious language can carry this heavy cultic overtone. Once, when interviewing a former member of the Church of Bible Understanding, I remarked that she looked "blue." To my surprise she began weeping and ran out of the room. I later learned that the Church of Bible Understanding "color-coded" the Bible, assigning every verse a color according to its meaning. Apparently the color blue was reserved for passages dealing with sin, guilt, and death. I had inadvertently told this woman she looked "sinful," even "dead"!

RELEARNING BASIC MEANINGS

We must help the ex-member learn (or relearn) the basic Christian meaning of religious terms. Forcing this reeducation process upon the ex-member would be akin to using the manipulative tactics of the cult leaders. Rather, sensitivity to the readiness of the ex-cultist is important in gradually helping him or her rediscover the true meaning of such terms as "saved," "born-again," "Christian," and "love," as well as the doctrines and symbols of the church. Because of the cults' insidious practices of twisting the Scriptures, many Bible passages must be reinterpreted. A Bible scholar's short course in hermeneutics, (the science of Bible interpretation) may be helpful to an ex-member. Many sectarian groups and all cults practice very skewed, peculiar hermeneutics that bolster their unique religious ideas.

As strange as it may seem, the ex-cultist must be aided in *redeeming* Christian language and the words of the Holy Scriptures. Until this process is complete, he or she is cut off from the work of the Holy Spirit through God's Word. The proper understanding of the Word is a means of grace. This is the awful terror of cultic religious ideas—that God's very Word is covered with a film, a layer of lies and perversions that prevent the ex-member from understanding it for what it is. Opening such blinded eyes will require prayer, deep commitment to the task, genuine humility, and sensitivity to both the ex-cultist and the Holy Spirit who convicts, guides, and teaches.

THE CHRISTIAN COMMUNITY

Part of being a friend to the ex-cultist will naturally include an invitation to attend a Christian fellowship. That invitation should be low-key, with no attempt toward coercion into church activities such as Sunday school or membership training classes, or baptism into the full fellowship of the church. The Holy Spirit will take over the work through His workshop, the church, and through His temples, Christian people.

This relaxed approach should preclude the tendency to treat the ex-cultist as a spiritual "coup" another "scalp" to hang on an evangelical belt. The ex-member is a person with dignity—not a freak, a spectacle, a public display of someone's evangelistic talents.

COMING HOME

In time, through the church's outreach of friendship and love, and patient teaching of the Bible, theology, and explaining of cultic practices, the ex-member may be brought to self-knowledge and to acceptance of Christianity again. Considerate treatment of the ex-member, however, will speak much louder than words.

Meanwhile, when the ex-cultist has been warmed by love and inspired by the Holy Spirit, he or she will want to become a part of a church fellowship. All should be welcomed as children of God, into the full fellowship of the one holy, catholic, and apostolic church.

NOT YET THE KINGDOM

The church, the healing fellowship, can only function best when it is not laden with sectarianism, a Pharisee-like behavior that builds a wall separating the people inside the church from those on the outside. In order to preserve the purity of their gospel, sectarian groups prohibit relationships with other Christian, civic, or secular groups. This kind of congregation, with its elitism and moralism, often exhibits strong prejudice toward anyone who isn't "theirs." Healing is not only prevented, but divisions and schisms between individuals and groups are provoked. Such judgmentalism is squarely contrary to Jesus' injunction in the Sermon on the Mount, "Judge not, that you be not judged" (Matt. 7:1).

Such congregations are rarely able to help ex-cultists or other victims of sin and crime. A healing fellowship must exhibit tolerance, openness, and acceptance of everyone, without regard to race, color, lifestyle, previous religious experience, or behavior. Christ excludes no one.

YOU ARE ACCEPTED

The Christian message may be briefly summarized in John 3:16: "For God so loved the world that he gave his only Son, that whoever believes in him should . . . have eternal life."

To summarize the gospel in even fewer words: "You are acceptable. You are accepted."

God loved the world so much that, before our births, indeed, even before the foundation of the world, He determined to save us from our sins. This overwhelming *agape,* the mystery of salvation, was manifested when Christ died in your place to save you and all sinners who will repent and turn to Him.

That is the message of the cross. That is the true content of the Christian invitation. Every great preacher—from Peter and Paul to Athanasius, Augustine, Francis of Assisi, Martin Luther, John Calvin, John Wesley, Paul Tillich, Karl Barth, Emil Brunner, Reinhold Niebuhr, to Carl Henry and Billy Graham—has proclaimed that same basic invitational message.

ACCEPTING OTHERS

Remember that profoundly wonderful truth: In all our sinfulness, we are accepted. The only necessary response is: accepting acceptance. The drug addict, the dope peddler, the alcoholic, the adulterer, the thief, the pornographer, the white-collar criminal and, yes, the ex-cultist who once believed that Moses David was the "end-time prophet" or that the Maharaji-Ji was God—all are accepted. No sin is greater than any other; no sinner worse than others. All sin separates from God. The Cross puts all believing sinners on an equal footing—in relationship with God. We are accepted. They are accepted. We need to give the Holy Spirit time to heal open wounds.

From the perspective of faith, the presence of ex-cultists in our Christian fellowships may be viewed as God's gracious invitation to revitalize our churches. The opportunity to minister humbly and lovingly to ex-cultists may enable us to transform our congregations into the true "hospitals for souls" they were intended to be.

My experience reveals that "liberal" congregations are able to integrate the ex-cultist into the life of the church more often than are "conservative" congregations. Welcoming all kinds of people into the church seems to be the human key to a problem that has, at last, a divine solution.

HOW TO START A CLASS ON CULTS

The presence of an ex-cultist in the church may spark among church members a lively curiosity about cults, sometimes spontaneously resulting in special interest groups. Such groups are ideal platforms from which to provide nurture, fellowship and a receptive climate for the ex-cultist, as well as disseminate valuable information to the church.

The following suggestions may be helpful:

1. *Invite a responsible speaker* (possibly an ex-cultist) to a church service, Sunday school, or informal church gathering. An interesting lecture by an authority on cults or by a former cult member will form the basis for the study group.

2. *Provide sound study materials.* The subject of the "new religions" is an emotional minefield, full of charges

and countercharges by both cultists and anticultists. Books, articles, tapes, and films produced by either of these extremists are not helpful for those seeking objectivity and truth, and may cause divisions and confusion. It is because of the extremist, sensational, and erroneous nature of much of the popular literature on cults that the authors and publishers have produced the present volume.

Denominational publishing houses may be able to supply study materials on the cults. Broadman Press (a division of the Baptist Sunday School Board), Abingdon Press (a division of the United Methodist Publishing House), Judson Press, Westminster Press, Fortress Press, and other church sponsored publishers will supply you with books you can trust.

3. *Carefully monitor discussions and conclusions.* Don't allow your class to degenerate into a series of horror stories about the new religions or anti-cult deprogrammers. A study of the *whys* —why people join cults and why cults arise in the first place—is much more important. Exploring the Bible and studying the resources of your faith can help determine how to prevent fellow believers from joining cults. This is the real purpose and value of such a class.

4. *Encourage the larger church* (conference, synod, association, district, or denomination) to take the presence of cults seriously. Church officials need the plight of ex-cultists brought to their attention through phone calls, resolutions, and letters, urging the establishment of task forces on cult-related problems.

As public awareness is raised outside the church, attention will be focused on the widespread despair of parents, spouses, friends, and relatives of people drawn into the cults. Rather than acting as another pressure group, Christian people, following the model of the One who practiced peace, can bring a spirit of understanding to entire communities. A new attitude toward the cults and ex-cultists comes only from a humble, serving heart.

9. A Call to the Church

Undoubtedly, there is no single, sure way to protect the young, who are precisely seeking for an identity, feel insecure and find it difficult to tell the genuine from the false. But there are some things we can bear in mind. Among them:

Remember that even Christian families are vulnerable to the lure of Bible-based cults. The cults are looking for idealistic young people who are searching for meaning in their lives. Their tactics are most successful with people who have a nominal church background.

The cults capitalize on real unmet spiritual needs. Young people who are sincerely devoted to Jesus Christ and the church and have the support of a strong, loving family are not as liable to be attracted to cults. Unfortunately, we must face up to the fact that family life is not as strong as it could be. Regular church attendance by young people may not be as high in the urban areas where the cults are most active as it is in rural areas where there is less cult activity.

We must recall that the condition of the American family is very much an issue in the rise and attractiveness of cults. There is a crisis in America that has much to do with the lack of a strong authority figure in many families. Charismatic cult leaders function as substitute father figures and are attractive to both young men and women. They are often even called father, either officially or informally.

Cults attract individuals, not families, as a rule. Being together as a family, therefore, particularly in religious matters, is an important preventive against cult exploitation.

Grant R. Osborne, writing in the June 29, 1979, issue of *Christianity Today*, mentions five ways to counter the cultic curse. His principles are summarized below:

1. The Jesus principle. We should beware of wolves in sheep's clothing. In John 10 Jesus referred to wolves who would destroy and the self-centered hireling who would not protect the sheep. The first principle, then, is to examine our leaders and discern when self-interest or false teaching begins to erode their ideals. The church should never assume that a great leader will always make correct decisions.

2. The principles of Acts. In Acts 17:11 the Berean Christians were described as those who . . . "received the message with great eagerness and examined the Scriptures every day to see if what Paul said was true" (NIV). We must prepare this type of layperson, eager for the Word—yet desiring to examine it for himself/herself before accepting the truth of a statement. We must examine the message of every preacher and measure it against the Bible.

3. Paul's approach. Paul, in his epistles (1 Corinthians 15:3–5; 2 Timothy 2:2), emphasizes the importance of tradition in the church as a control against aberrations. Knowledge of Scripture and of the historic creeds of the church would warn us against many of the new groups that teach very old heresies, such as Arianism in the Jehovah's Witnesses and The Way and libertinism in the Children of God and People's Temple.

4. The Johannine formulae. In 1 John there are two criteria for distinguishing true teachers from false. The first is their ethics. If a ministry is characterized by a self-centered lifestyle rather than a love-centered servant attitude, then it is subject to question. The second test is the message. The leader's message must square with traditional Christian belief in the incarnation and deity of Jesus Christ.

5. The method in Jude and 2 Peter. These two books tell us that we must confront and repudiate false teachers and

lovingly restore those who have been swayed by heretical teachings. Of course, we need to be careful that we use the term heresy only for the central doctrines of Christendom, such as the Trinity, the Person of Christ, and salvation through Christ. We are not to revive the modernist-funda-mentalist dispute or argue over modes of baptism. There are some doctrines that we must struggle to keep and others that genuinely Christian people may disagree on in love.

In addition to Osborne's suggestions for countering cults, we must consider legal ways to control deceptive recruiting practices and behavioral conditioning techniques of indoctrination that violate human rights. And above all, we must devise ways to control the solicitation of money in the name of all religious groups—mainline, fundamentalist, and cultic.

If cults are blocked in their deceptive recruiting efforts, they can only shrink. If they are blocked in their deceptive money-making schemes, then their gurus and preachers will switch to something else. For underneath all the biblical research and vestments, in each of these cultic groups there is a bright green idol called Money. But if it were only money they were after, we could live with them as we do with greedy advertisers, unscrupulous used car salesmen, and shady politicians. But cult leaders want money because, ultimately, it is power they really want— first, over a few people, and then over everyone, if they can get it! That's why we must fight this new form of spiritual fascism even if it does come carrying a Bible and promising salvation.

Appendix A— Historical Perspective on Cults

Over the last several decades many new and different forms of religious expression have surfaced in North America. Some of these religious expressions have been calls for a return to older forms of spirituality or for modern interpretations of traditional doctrines. Other groups have arisen in response to the growing involvement of the United States with the Far East. Sincere attempts to translate Buddhism and Hinduism into an American idiom have been made. Still other groups have sprung up with the growing awareness that the industrialized countries have wasted natural resources and polluted our planet. Finally, popular psychologies stressing self-awareness and fulfillment have provoked spiritual expressions which commentator Thomas Wolfe refers to as being part of the "me generation" mentality.

It would be difficult to say just how many such groups operate in America today. Educated guesses run from several hundred to five thousand—with a total of ten to fifteen million members. Whatever the number, there are enough forms of new religious expression to make us all aware that contemporary religion encompasses more than services-as-usual at the corner church.

Some of the "new forms" of spirituality have been fairly well accepted. These forms are actually renewed emphasis by the church on the gifts of the Spirit and spiritual disciplines. In many cases, local groups that teach and worship in this manner are not considered cults by even the most biased outsiders. This is a true appraisal, for they are but local churches, perhaps viewed as fanatical or far-fetched by the world or even by fellow Christians, but sincerely seeking to follow biblical principles. However, such groups that appear to entertain an unbalanced emphasis upon one biblical principle above the others may attract suspicion and bad press.

While not technically correct, speakers and writers have tended to use the word "cult" to apply to any form of spiritual expression that has not been fully accepted.

For our own clarification, let's carefully define "cult" so we can separate "suspicious" groups from dangerous cults.

Appendix B—
Definition of Cult

Most of us take religion for granted. The average person belongs, at least in a nominal sense, to a church or synagogue. On any Sunday morning, millions of us are in church or church schools, while Saturdays find Jews, Sabbatarian Christians, and Catholics at worship. Many others at least attend services on Easter and Christmas or the Jewish high holy days.

In our free society, some find organized religion irrelevant, but only a few Americans are actually hostile toward or militantly opposed to religion. We live in a secular, but not atheistic, society. We might characterize it as pluralistically religious.

Then one morning we are stunned by the headlines and news reports of the Jonestown massacre. Murder and suicide, sex, and revolution are not elements of the religion our society views as wholesome and harmless as apple pie. I have no desire to recite the story of Rev. Jones and the bizarre, demented horror of Jonestown. Yet Jim Jones and the People's Temple are not unique phenomena in the America of the last twenty years. This is only one of a large number of new, unusual, and fast-growing religious groups that have become known as cults. Whatever cults are, by their very nature and size, they are significant elements of the current national scene.

There are many differences of opinion as to just what constitutes a cult. Some groups, such as the International Society for Krishna Consciousness, have circulated material denying that they are cults. Of course, any definition and identification of the teaching and practice of values and beliefs is always relative.

Yet the word "cult" begs for a definition. We need some

boundaries set around the concept so that we can measure a group and objectively determine whether or not it deserves such a label.

In his book *Scientific Study of Religion,* J. Milton Yinger defines cults as:

> . . . religious mutants . . . a group at the farthest extreme from the "universal church" . . . usually small, short-lived, local, and built around a charismatic leader.

W. W. Sweet, in *American Culture and Religion,* holds that cults are:

> . . . religious groups which look for their basic and peculiar authority outside the Christian tradition. Generally, cults accept Christianity but often only as a halfway station on the road to a brighter "truth" and profess to have a new, and additional authority beyond Christianity.

Appendix C—
Characteristics of the
Destructive Cults

During the last several years, John Cooper has studied the various movements called cults in the United States and has investigated this phenomenon in Canada, Mexico, Europe, Korea, and North Africa. He has been privileged to interview both cult members and former cult members—alone, in groups, even in "rest houses" following deprogramming. On the basis of his conversations, he has developed a list of characteristics that readily identify the kind of "cult" or "new religion" that raises—and should raise—fear and suspicion in discerning minds. By some commentators this type of group is called a "destructive cult."

Surprisingly (or not so surprisingly, depending upon one's theological orientation), in their organization, belief, systems, and attitudes cults are similar to the ultra-conservative wing of Christianity. In fact, any branch of the universal church that Jesus established on earth shares some characteristics with the cults. Therefore, consider this a warning: The boundaries between truth and distortion are hazily defined. Those spiritual seekers who have a fanatical frame of reference with a questionable foundation of faith are most vulnerable to cultic persuasion. Only when we understand the marks of the cults can we begin to oppose them.

The first four elements listed are characteristics that destructive cults share with some churches, but our different motives make a world of difference.

1. *A realistic apocalypticism.* The world is coming to an end soon. This period will involve great tribulation (such as the fall of America), a worldwide atomic war, or the onset of the biblical plagues mentioned in Revelation. Everything

is viewed in extreme, radical terms: Repent now and flee the wrath to come. World events, particularly in the Middle East, are seen as definite signs of impending disaster from which only the faithful will escape. This teaching is found in all cults, whether of Eastern, Hindu, or Christian background. (The Divine Light Mission announced the advent of the Millennium and was seriously damaged when nothing happened.) While each group gives its own particular twist to this "end time," there is little distinction between the doomsayers within some churches and cultic prophets.

2. *Polemics against all other groups.* Cults attack the "false theology" of main-line Protestant churches and the Roman Catholic church, for there is a large element of anti-clericalism in all cultic movements.

3. *Aggressive proselytizing.* Most cult groups seem to exist for the sole purpose of making new members.

4. *High-demand commitment.* A high demand is made on the new member's time, commitment, and material possessions.

The following marks are unique to cults. Any group characterized by one or more of these is certainly not any part of the Christian church:

5. *Heavy behavioral conditioning.* The indoctrination of new members into a cult group is accomplished through isolation, deprivation, conditioning, and other forms of behavior modification.

6. *Total loyalty to one person.* Almost without exception, cults are marked by absolute, unquestioning allegiance to one person.

7. *Economic and personal exploitation.* Members are treated as being "means" to an end—the financial security of the leaders. These recruits often live under the most austere of conditions, while cult officials live comfortably or even luxuriously. Vows of poverty are intended only for the devotees. Some excultists have disclosed that they

have begged as much as $30,000 a year, only to turn all funds over to the cult authorities.

Personal exploitation is even more demeaning. Jim Jones' sexual exploitation of both men and women in the People's Temple is not unique. The classical cult configuration includes sexual license, from the witch cults to the early Mormons to the Children Of God/Family of Love who train young men and women to become "hookers for Jesus," using sex as a means of recruiting new converts.

8. *Heavenly deception.* Cults are marked by the practice of deception in all their dealings, both with members and with outsiders.

The Citizens Freedom Foundation — Information Services, a group that coordinates the national grassroots anticult associations, offers their own definition of a destructive cult as being "under the control of an authoritarian leader by means of deceptive practices and psychological manipulation. Mind control is established and maintained for the leader's power and wealth."

The dangers of the destructive cults are two-fold: They fill a person's spiritual void with a false theology, and they violate the psychological, mental, and even physical rights of men and women by breaking down the harmony that God would choose to establish and sustain.

If we criticize the cultist, we must also criticize the churches. Many people entering cults are making sincere confessions of faith in God and, in the Western-oriented cults, in Jesus Christ as well.

Why people join cults is as broad an area of investigation as religion itself. Humanity has a need to believe, a bent toward becoming twice-born. And, unfortunately, there are thousands of religious type who know the psychological mechanisms that can provoke the "new birth" experience in the lonely seeker.

Within Jesus' call to commitment and the appropriate responses that have been hallowed among us for centuries, we rejoice with the expressed desire of a loved one to deepen his faith, to accept the challenge to the spiritual life. But let us guard against filling spiritual voids through membership in cults. Knowledge about the specific cults is one of the best safeguards.

Appendix D—
Specific Cults Explained

A CULT WITH NO NAME
("THE GARBAGE EATERS")

This nomadic cult was apparently begun in 1969, founded by Jimmie T. Roberts, a native of Kentucky, who graduated last in his 1958 high-school class.

Roberts, who calls himself "Brother-Evangelist," leads his band of less than a hundred across the United States. They drift about in long robes, seldom wash, and pray fervently. In their wake is a trail of broken homes and battered women and children.

The Scripture teachings Roberts advocates include frantic discipline of children and women, citing the Scripture: "The rod and reproof give wisdom" (Prov. 29:15 KJV). The group is convinced that the world is imminently facing the end destruction, and, because children are too young to know God, they are ruled by Satan. By this reasoning, beating a child is whipping Satan.

The cult, which has no headquarters, is sometimes called "The Garbage Eaters," because of their habit of sorting through restaurant trash bins for food.

Many of Roberts' followers are college students searching for identity and for something in which they can believe. Influenced by his almost hypnotic power, these members obey Roberts' every word and believe that disobedience would bring them eternal damnation.

THE CHURCH OF ARMAGEDDON
(THE LOVE FAMILY)

Paul Erdmann is founder and self-proclaimed leader of the Church of Armageddon, which began in 1969 in Seattle. By

1972 the church owned seven houses in Seattle, and now also has a small colony on the island of Hawaii.

This group of several hundred claims that the church was founded to "fulfill the New Testament as revealed to Love Israel [Erdmann's self-given name] in the form of visions, dreams, and revelations received by members of the church. The members of the church have all had heavenly visions. . . ."

The name, Church of Armageddon, is taken from Revelation 16:16, in which Armageddon is mentioned as the end-time gathering place. Members also refer to themselves as the Love Family, and state in their charter: "The Kingdom of God is a state of love, a family that can never end, the Love Family. Our family surname is Israel. Our duty is to show mankind that Love is real."

The church claims to be the continuation of Israel (Old Testament) and to follow the true beliefs of Jesus Christ (New Testament). It practices baptism by immersion and believes that all eating and drinking is sacramental—whatever is eaten is the body of Christ and whatever is drunk is the blood of Christ. Members shun outside medical care, following the teachings of Erdmann's book, *Love*.

Love Israel governs the church and is assisted by a governor, Serious Israel, and a chief captain, Strength Israel.

Joining the church represents freeing oneself from a past life of sin and death. New members are expected to give all they possess and take a new name, with the common surname, Israel, since Israel is the name of God's people. A "virtue" name is assumed as a first name.

New members are expected to renounce all "worldly traditions of matrimony," as the church reasons that, as one body, the church is married to Christ, individually and collectively, and members are married to one another in Christ. The three top leaders, however, have authority to allow "bonding" by couples, for the purpose of having children. In these relationships, the men have authority over the women.

CHURCH OF BIBLE UNDERSTANDING

First known as the Forever Family, this cult began in 1971 in Allentown, Pennsylvania, headed by Stewart Traill.

The Church of Bible Understanding is a classic example of the "Bible cult," using much of the same terminology of orthodox Christianity, but assigning unorthodox meaning. This group claims to be in fellowship with Jesus and His Word—to be orthodox, catholic, and apostolic in doctrine, and to be bold, open, and direct in speaking the gospel.

However, they believe that the Bible's meaning was concealed until Traill came along to reveal it. All other churches have been unfaithful, they claim, and they are the restoration of the true church because of their exclusive possession of true "Bible understanding"—only Traill's teachings are God's truth for today.

Their interpretation of the Bible is allegorical and highly subjective, making use of a "figure system," in which the surface understanding of the Bible is explored to reveal the true and deeper meaning through "figures," words that are replaced with another word of "true" meaning. Traill remains the sole authority on these true meanings.

They reject the orthodox view of the Trinity, believing that the Son is lower than the Father, and that the Holy Spirit is yet another step lower.

The church claims to have declared war on the powers of this world, including government, police, schools, parents, big business, press, employers, neighborhoods, churches, friends, society, and most older persons.

Church members work up to eighteen hours a day witnessing, attempting to contact teenagers who are disoriented or estranged from their parents. Once lured into the cult, such young people are forced by the use of scare tactics into staying. They are told stories of people who have left the cult only to be killed or suffer some other tragedy.

Traill himself is revered and given absolute control. His word is law and members believe statements made by those outside the cult are influenced by the Devil. Sometimes described as obnoxious and scornful, Traill has little positive regard for the members. He has been known to show up to speak some four or five hours late and then launch a degrading attack on the members in attendance.

The church grew from six members to a high of three thousand in 1976, and has now dwindled to about seven hundred members. The group is especially concentrated in nine Eastern states—in the cities of Philadelphia, New York, Washington, Boston, and Cleveland, and has a mission of about forty people in Haiti. Members contribute their entire paychecks to the church, with little explanation given as to how it will be used.

CHILDREN OF GOD

Fundamentalist groups made the tract a recognizable tool for religious recruitment generations ago. In more recent years the Jesus People movements have made comic books a part of their evangelism techniques. But no acquaintance with popular religious literature will prepare you for the "witnessing" material of the Family of Love, better known as the Children of God.

These curious little pamphlets, sold diligently on street corners incongruously picture the prophet of the group, Moses David, born David Brant Berg, naked in bed with unclothed, well-endowed women, receiving revelations from God through dreams. These dreams, which Berg claims are spirit messages that come to him from discarnate intelligences, give bizarre new twists to conventional Christian teachings. Perhaps the most widely known example of Berg's teaching is that since God is love and sex is called love, then the Children of God ought to use sex to show God's love to the world. Some of Berg's pamphlets, quite frankly, are more pornographic than any of the cartoons or articles in the March 1980 issue of *Hustler* magazine, which reproduced them in an article by George Hill entitled "Religious Sex Cult." Within one of Berg's pamphlets is a continuing series of erotic drawings with the legend, "In as much as she has done it unto the *least* of these my brethren, she has done it unto *me*." This last phrase is accompanied by a drawing that shows the man turning into the Lord Jesus.

Berg's obsession with sex goes back a long way. In fact, John Cooper's first encounter with the Children of God was when he was given a double pamphlet on a street corner in Edmonton, Alberta, Canada, in 1973. The pamphlet included "End Time Rhyme" and "Mountain Maid," an odd poem copyrighted by the Children of God Trust that celebrates sexual relations and calls upon women to stop wearing bras. At the time he received the pamphlet he thought it was a piece of pornography rather than a religious tract. Compared to more recent pamphlets, this earlier piece of literature was sedate.

The seeds for the beginning of the Children of God were planted in 1968 in Huntington Beach, California, when Rev. David Berg, former Christian and Missionary Alliance minister who had left that denomination, became leader of a Teen Challenge unit. He and his family took over a coffee house ministry and focused their attention on young people, many of whom were involved with the drug culture.

Berg stressed Bible study among his little flock and began to preach against the "system" and the nation. In the late 1960s Berg joined a host of psychics in predicting that California would be hit by an earthquake and fall into the Pacific Ocean. Twice he said he "knew" the exact time and led his followers to the mountains for safety. California did not move. Berg did. He shut down the coffee house, split his band into groups and went across the nation proclaiming doom and judgment and recruiting.

In 1969 the separated groups were together again wandering their way to Texas. Berg gave them the idea that they were like Moses and the Israelites in the wilderness. Correspondingly, they took biblical names, Berg becoming Moses David. Their communes were given Hebrew tribal names and the entire group took on the name Children of God, a name the press had been using that Berg liked and decided to keep.

Years before, Berg had gone to California as a public relations man for Fred Jordan, head of the American Soul Clinic and TV's "Church in the Home." Now Jordan gave Berg and his colonies the use of three Jordan properties, one in New Thurber, Texas, one in Coachella, California, and a five-story building in downtown Los Angeles.

The set-up with Jordan was short-lived, however, and in the fall of 1971 the COG colonies were evicted. That only served to spread the group. They went to San Diego, Seattle, Detroit, Dallas, Austin, New York, Vancouver, and many other places, picking up converts, especially among the Jesus People movement. In Seattle, Linda Meisner of the Jesus People Army joined up, bringing some of her followers. Russ Griggs joined the COG and brought his flock. David Hoyt, who later left the COG and became an outspoken opponent of COG, joined Berg in Atlanta and brought four of his communes with him.

Berg also began to send missionaries and colonies overseas. The first mission was by one of Berg's daughters in 1971. Soon colonies were made across Western Europe. By 1977 the group claimed 7,500 American members, with 7,000 of those in mission colonies in seventy-two countries. In 1977 there were sixty colonies in the United States. The American headquarters is in Chicago.

In 1972 Richard Nixon was re-elected as President and Berg decided it was time to "get out of Babylon." Many of the COG took vacations to other lands—and just never came back.

In 1974 and 1975 Berg began to break down his large

Dealing With Destructive Cults

colonies into smaller ones, thus taking away the influence of certain persons. There are now seven levels of leadership in the group. No colony is to have more than twelve members. When the thirteenth arrives the colony is to be split in two.

Berg promotes hatred in the movement—hatred for the system, the society, parents, government, churches, and education. Naturally, COG has picked up many enemies along the way. A Parents' Committee to Free Our Children from the Children of God was organized in San Diego, claiming that COG kept its members through brainwashing techniques and hypnotism. Newspapers began publishing illuminating articles about the techniques and the immorality of the group.

Another twist came to the group in 1970, when Berg was introduced in Houston to a group of gypsies who enabled Berg to communicate with dead spirits. In his "MO letters," believed by his followers to be the inspired word of God for today, Berg claims to have spirit friends like Ivan the Terrible, Rasputin, William Jennings Bryan, Joan of Arc, Oliver Cromwell, and Abrahim the Gypsie King. (FN [MO letter, No. 296] GP, April 30, 1970).

Since that time Berg claims to have received instruction and guidance for the COG from these spirits, which seem to have led Berg to establish in the name of religion what George Hill calls, "one of the most successful international prostitution rings in history." (FN, George Hill, "Family of Love: Religious Sex Cult," *Hustler* [March 1980]: 70). Defectors from the Family of Love claim that both male and female members are required to perform all types of sexual acts for money. Apparently members are charged by Berg with the responsibility of having sex with potential converts or anyone else who might give funds for the group. The recruitment of these paying sexual partners is called "flirty-fishing."

The introduction of more and more sexual elements into the Children of God movement caused a number of members to question seriously why they should continue in the group. One of these increasingly disaffected members was Una McManus, a native of Dublin, Ireland, who fled from the cult when flirty-fishing became mandatory. Moving to the U. S. from a cult center in Scandinavia, Una was followed and her children taken by the man she married in the cult. She fought back and, after much litigation, got possession of her children again and won a civil suit against Moses David and the Children of God in the amount of one and a half million dollars. Judge William Gillie of the Franklin County Court of Common Pleas in Columbus, Ohio, made the award saying, "This court awards Una McManus one million dollars in compensatory damages and one-half million dollars in punitive damages against the Children of God religious cult and its leader David Brandt Berg, also known as Moses David, for alienation of her husband's affection, and for the misrepresentation of their ideals." Una's story is told in *Not for a Million Dollars* (Nashville: Impact Books, 1980).

Needless to say, she has not collected this money as the COG cult is underground and claims to own no property in America. Berg, if he is still living, is in hiding somewhere in Europe.

THE DIVINE LIGHT MISSION

The Divine Light Mission was begun in India by the famous guru, Paran Sant Satgurudev Shri Hans Ji Maharaj, some forty years before its appearance in the United States in 1971.

The guru's son, Maharaj Ji, had begun making "discourses" to his family at age two, and soon afterward began making public speeches, giving his first speech in English at the age of six. Two years later, at his father's funeral, Maharaj Ji claims to have heard an "inner voice" tell him that he would be the next master. He made this announcement to the mourners, they fell prostrate at his feet to receive his blessing, and suddenly the child was the new leader of the Divine Light Mission.

In 1970, the thirteen-year-old guru proclaimed the dawning of a new age, and sent out a few of his staff to prepare the way for him. In 1972, he traveled to England and then to the U.S. Thanks to his abilities and well-planned advertising and media coverage, he was an instant success.

By the fall of 1972, centers (ashrams) were being established around the United States, and a meeting in Colorado claimed two thousand converts.

This movement springs from Hindu background, therefore teaching that God is impersonal, is in everything, and is the source of everything. This impersonal power has been incarnated into Vishu, Krishna, Jesus, Buddha, and a succession of Satgurus (perfect masters). Each age has only one Satguru, and Maharaj Ji is the Satguru for the present age.

Jesus, they say, was the living perfect master for His time. But we need a new living master for today—Maharaj Ji, the one who can lead us to salvation. Through the knowledge received from his teachings, and devotion of followers' lives to him, they can become united with the universe.

The DLM has been marked with wide variances in its teachings and beliefs. Prior to 1973, the appeal of the group revolved around the belief that Maharaj Ji was the Lord and that a new age of peace was to begin under his leadership. The failure of a meeting called "Millennium 1973," held at the Houston Astrodome, cost the group $600,000 and attracted only twenty thousand people instead of the hoped-for two hundred thousand. It also set off a crisis within the group and Maharaj Ji's family, with some persons beginning to frown on his expensive cars and lavish lifestyle

A long-standing feud between the guru and his mother broke into the open at this time, and resulted in the guru's defending himself as the sole authority, rejecting his mother. He also became more Westernized and approved the marriage of his brother to a German citizen who was living in the United States. Then he married Marolyn Lois Johnson, an American devotee eight years his senior, further souring the family. At this, his mother, Mata Ji, tried to remove him from control, but he rejected her attempts. The entire movement became more and more Western, eliminating many Indian traditions and rituals, and reducing the number and prestige of the Indian mahatmas. Many left the group, to be replaced by Western devotees.

With the removal of the Indian traditions came a change in attitude concerning Maharaj Ji's status. By 1975, the guru was generally viewed as a "humanitarian leader" rather than the Lord of the universe, and by 1976, he was regarded in human rather than divine terms.

Along with the demystification of DLM theology came a change in their style of leadership. Organization was decentralized and some decision-making power was given to local communities.

But since 1976, general DLM opinion has swung back to the belief that the guru is Lord of the universe, without whose help one can hardly make it through the day. Devotion, adoration, and worship have gone back to levels of the early days. Many novices in the movement (premies) are again returning to the premise that he is the Messiah, and are taking part in devotional singing and rituals.

The group is now more tolerant of variances in their members' belief and experience, but few changes have concerned "knowledge."

Premies are promised spiritual knowledge through practice of the meditation techniques. They are told to meditate for an hour morning and evening, giving complete service and submission to the guru—falling in love with him, and seeing God in him.

A mahatma shows a premie a secret means of seeing the divine inner light, hearing celestial noises, and tasting divine nectar. The new convert is taught to press the side of the forehead with thumb and middle finger, while pressing the lower center of the forehead with an index finger—thereby, seeing stars! The mahatma may press his fingers firmly into the premie's ears, causing the celestial sound (that of blood pulsing through the veins). The premie is taught to curl the tongue far back into the mouth and thereby taste the divine nectar (called post-nasal drip by the uninitiated) which is nourishment placed in the throat before birth. The DLM teaches that this was Jesus' source of nourishment during the forty days in the wilderness.

These three activities serve as preparations for the ultimate experience—that of a divine inner vibration, the Word. By meditating on the sound of one's own breath, the premie can "get the knowledge" promised by Maharaj Ji. Once the technique is mastered, the premie "blitzes out," experiencing an inner peace, which is union with God beyond time and space. This is an experience of infinity available through the body.

The premies are told that every human has four blessings—the privilege of being born in a human body, the holy scriptures of all religions, God's incarnation as a spiritual master, and one's own effort. Salvation is received when all four of these blessings are used and when one is completely devoted to the guru.

In 1977, the DLM reported fifty-thousand persons involved in the group, with ten thousand to twelve thousand of those very active in the work.

ECKANKAR

Eckankar was founded in 1964 by Paul Twitchell, a native Kentuckian and a graduate of Western Kentucky University. A free-lance writer and dabbler in Eastern religions and the occult, Twitchell had been for some time a full-time follower of Kirpal Singh in the Self-revelation Church of Absolute Monism and had served as a staff member of L. Ron Hubbard's Scientology movement in 1958.

Before his death (or "translation," according to Eckankar belief) in 1971, Twitchell declared Eckankar to be the most ancient religious tradition known to humanity—the path to total awareness; to becoming God, realized through the ancient science of soul travel. Further, Twitchell taught that entrance to heaven is attainable only through the teachings of Eckankar.

These teachings say that heaven is made up of eleven different planes: the upper six being heavenly and the lower five being ruled by negative divine forces symbolized by Kal, the Devil. The earthly world is the first plane and the second is the astral plane, the place of occult and psychic experiences.

It is believed that few disciples are able to take their believers beyond the lower planes, and the only way to rise upward to God (called Sugmad by Twitchell) is through soul travel. Only with the guidance of the living Eck Master or Mahanta, the chela (student) is plugged into the cosmic current (the Eck) and learns to go with the flow to reach progressive self-realization or God-realization.

Many forms of meditation involve contemplation of the Master, either in his physical or spiritual form. Through any of ten initiations which are earned by the student, the soul is translated upward from one plane to another. This involves soul travel, or out-of-the-body experiences, achieved by chanting mantras and other occult means of altering consciousness. The belief is that spirits are contacted along the way.

Through the practice of Eckankar, one may get off the Wheel of Eighty-four, or the wheel of reincarnation. This can be done only by following the Eck master, who is an avatar, or savior, in the traditional Hindu system. The Eckist believes that God is everything—nothing in the universe is not the Sugmad. This includes even Satan, who is called Kal Nirangan. This potential problem is solved with the explanation that Kal acts to purify the soul through temptation.

Sin is described with the Hindu term "bad Karma," and salvation may be obtained by working off the karmic debt. This debt is enlarged through the five passions of lust, anger, greed, undue attachment to material things, and vanity.

The Eckist soul goes through millions of reincarnations as it rises on the evolutionary scale of life. (Twitchell claimed to have started as a mineral eight million years ago.)

Today the group is directed by Sir Darwin Gross, who is called the 972nd Living Master.

INTERNATIONAL SOCIETY FOR KRISHNA CONSCIOUSNESS (HARE KRISHNA)

This group which gained U.S. popularity in the mid sixties, has roots in Hinduism and began as a popular sect in India in 1486. In 1965 Swami Abhay Charan De Bhaktivedanta Prabhupada, nearly seventy years of age, took a freighter from Calcutta to New York to spread the news about Lord Krishna.

After a slow start, the age of the flower children gave Prabhupada the boost he needed for the addition of disciples. He wandered the streets of Greenwich Village, picking up followers. He chanted in Washington Square Park and Tompkins Square Park, attracting the attention and participation of such well-known persons as former Zen Buddhist and poet Allen Ginsberg as well as lesser personalities. Beatle George Harrison wrote the Krishna-influenced song, "My Sweet Lord," and Prabhupada's popularity was enhanced by stories published in the *East Village Other* and the *Village Voice*.

Krishna consciousness spread to Amsterdam, Paris, Rome, Copenhagen, and England and became a hit in Haight-Ashbury. The rock musical "Hair" made use of the common mantra chant of the Krishnas in one of its songs.

In 1968, Prabhupada began mass distribution of his magazine, *Back to Godhead,* which he had begun in 1944.

Krishna centers began to open up across the continental U.S. and George Harrison was among many who continued to support the group with music, money, and land. Alfred Ford, Henry Ford's great-grandson, paid leases on the group's California warehouses and lent money for the purchase of the Fisher Mansion. Lisa Reuther, the late labor leader Walter Reuther's daughter, donated her inheritance toward this same purchase.

By 1970 ISKCON claimed to have twenty-two centers in the United States, and, by 1972, counted three thousand in membership. Prabhupada died in 1977 and leadership of the organization passed to a twenty-two-member "governing body commission."

ISKCON resents being labeled a "new religion" or cult, claiming to be part of four thousand years of Hinduism. But the group's theology is both like and unlike most Hinduism. It differs in that its members worship Sod (Krishna) as a personal not an impersonal, force. Prabhupada derived this belief from his interpretation of the *Bhagavad-Gita,* the Hindu doctrinal book, which features Krishna. Prabhupada's version of the *Bhagavad-Gita* is the group's Bible.

Krishna, who first appeared on earth five thousand years ago, has had some twenty-five incarnations and is a personal, playful god, who is everything, everywhere.

In Prabhupada's teachings, the reality of a human being is the soul; the body is a source of spiritual problems and requires discipline. Reincarnation is a fact, and the purpose of life is the attainment of Krishna consciousness, the rebuilding of the forgotten relationship with him. This is accomplished by chanting the Hare Krishna mantra. Once one has Krishna consciousness, one lives by the pure rules of devotional service.

The life of the devotee is highly disciplined. Krishnas rise at 3:00 A.M., bathe, dress in clean clothes, and begin chants with the assistance of prayer beads. Services at 4:00 A.M. are followed by more individual chanting and 6:00 A.M.

study classes on the *Bhagavad-Gita* and other scriptures. Temple cleaning follows a 7:30 breakfast, putting the devotees on the street soliciting by 10:00. With only a brief lunch break, the soliciting lasts until 6:00 P.M. After evening showers (cleanliness is greatly stressed), a study hour, an evening service, and a class period are conducted. Hot milk is served around 8:15, followed by study and care of the temple idols. Much attention is given to washing temple statues with rose water, honey, milk, and cow's urine. Afterwards, devotees are honored to drink this liquid. Lights are out at 10:00 P.M. No more than six hours of sleep is allowed.

The robes worn by devotees symbolize renunciation of material pleasures. Women wear Indian saris; men wear dhotis—white for the married and saffron for the celibate unmarried. Men's heads are shaved except for a shika, a top knot by which Lord Krishna can pull them up to heaven.

Their strict Hindu dietary laws forbid the eating of meat, fish, or eggs, the drinking of coffee, tea, or cola, and the use of drugs and tobacco. About half the Krishnas are married but marriage is arranged by the group. Outside marriage is forbidden, and, if permission is given for two devotees to marry they are allowed sexual intercourse once a month on a night designated in the vedas for fertility. Sexual activity is preceded by five or six hours of chanting. Couples do not live together, and no divorce is allowed.

Women are considered subservient to all men and are forbidden to look a man in the eye—expected, instead, to look at his feet. Men eat first and women get the leftovers. A Boston temple leader teaches that men's brains weigh twice as much as women's.

Children are not allowed to attend public schools, but attend Krishna boarding schools called guru Kalas.

Chanting is basic to the Krishna lifestyle. By this devotion (called bhakti yoga—way of devotion—in Hindu theology) one supposedly receives the pure consciousness of God, in his prime incarnation of Krishna, and dispels the illusion which fills the world.

Members gladly practice sankirtana (chanting on the streets) to publish and sell Prabhupada's writings, including *Back to Godhead*. The deceptive nature of this sidewalk solicitation grows increasingly worse. Devotees now generally wear conventional clothes, including wigs for the men, to increase their acceptance, and have been known to dress as Santa Claus or the Easter bunny. During the Bicentennial a number wore cowboy hats and represented themselves as collecting for the Bicentennial Committee. Each brings in as much as $100 a day.

Other outward expressions of devotion include marking the body with clay in twelve places (Telok), public dancing (Kirtan), and eating prasadam, food offered to Krishna.

In recent years, the activities of devotees at airports have been restricted by judges and the public has grown aware of the "transcendental trickery" and short-changing practices of Krishnas. Neighbors of the Krishna shrine in West Virginia have grown disturbed since 1973, when the devotees began stockpiling arms and ammunition, claiming they are for self-defense.

Krishna officials claim to have about ten to twelve thousand initiated full-time members in forty temples in the United States, and more than one hundred centers abroad. They own more than twenty large urban properties and operate six farms in the United States and others abroad. ISKCON operates several businesses, including restaurants in Los Angeles, Hawaii, New York, Amsterdam, London, and Iran. In keeping with their vegetarian tradition, they sell Hare Krishna cookbooks and run a food-catering service in the Los Angeles area. They also make "Spiritual Sky Incense."

Dealing With Destructive Cults

THE UNIFICATION CHURCH (THE "MOONIES")

The Unification Church (the "Moonies") was born in the persecution and poverty of Korea during the Korean Conflict of 1954. Founded by the Reverend Sun Myung Moon, the movement spread to Japan, the U.S., and Europe, now reaching more than 120 nations and claiming thirty-thousand American followers, ten thousand of whom live in its religious communities.

The establishment of the new church was in response to a vision Moon experienced at the age of sixteen, in 1936, while praying in the mountains of his native North Korea. He claims to have been told by Jesus that he had been selected to carry out an important mission—assuming responsibility for completing Christ's unfinished task.

Through a series of revelations and communications with Christ, Moses, Buddha, and God, Moon claims to understand the nature of the universe, the meaning of history, and the "inner meanings" of biblical parables and symbols.

Though his followers represent him as not claiming to be the Messiah, Moon's criteria for the Messiah are fulfilled in his life. His birth date, place of birth, and marriage match the specifications he himself has set forth for the "Third Adam." (Jesus was the "Second Adam.")

Moon sees the role of the Third Adam as completing the work, begun, but not successfully achieved, by Jesus—the full physical as well as spiritual salvation of humanity. Moon—the Third Adam—will live a perfect life, establish a perfect family, and save the body as well as the soul.

Moon's basic theme is that humankind can not be restored to obedience to God while religion is fragmented into different groups. The task at hand is to unite the world through the Unification Church.

Moon's call for unity involves the need to evolve a social order of "worldwide socialist theocracy." Church and state, theology and science, economy and religion, are to be united under the Messiah and restored to God as one harmonious family.

In order to make his claims work, Moon has willingly "remodeled" Christianity considerably. Jesus' status is reduced from perfect and full Savior to "elder Brother," because of His lack of understanding of the Fall and the history of restoration. "Unless you truly know the meaning behind it, the Bible can reveal very little. . . . The Divine Principle [his own] gives the true meaning of the secret behind the verse," writes Moon in *Master Speaks*. Thus, the Bible is a cryptogram, and Moon's specially revealed wisdom is needed to correctly understand it.

The problem the Moonies claim to attack is humanity's original sin, defined as Eve's fornication with Lucifer and the passing of sin to Adam through sexual intercourse, which severed man's relationship with God.

Their solution is the establishment of true, pure love relations through submission (as to a father) to Moon, the True Parent and founder of the Perfect Family, on which the restoration of God's relations are to be based.

Meanwhile, the Moonies look for the new Messiah, to be revealed in the 1980s when the spirits of all who have ever lived will join Moon to develop divine spirits.

The Unification Church came to the United States in 1959, with Moon visiting in 1965 and 1969. In 1971, Moon moved to the U.S. and revised his teachings, making America a vital part of his millennial thinking. The U.S. was to be a new "archangel," and its support of the "new Adam" (Korea) and the "new Eve" (Japan) would undo the evil done by Lucifer when he broke humanity's harmony with God and with one another.

On this basis, Moon urges the U.S. to defeat Communism, to establish the order intended by God. America is thus a chosen nation, fitting Moonie doctrine neatly into a major theme of American civil or cultural religion.

From the beginning, Moon's organization has provided for business enterprises and the creation of wealth along with missionary outreach. The Moonies have concentrated on selling items, asking for donations, and investing in businesses. These clean-cut, well-dressed young people are ever-present on street corners, in airports—anywhere that people gather in America.

They try to sell such items as pamphlets, peanuts, candy, candles, American flags, and flowers, but usually do not identify themselves. Instead they tell the donor that the donation is for "a good cause," "missionary work," or "aiding drug addicts"—rarely identifying the Unification Church.

One Moonie was quoted as saying: "Satan deceived God's children, so we are justified in deceiving Satan's children." But this "heavenly deception" is more than a slogan. The Unification Church is adept at hiding their operations behind such front organizations as: One World Crusade, International Federation for Victory over Communism, American Youth for a Just Peace, Freedom Leadership Foundation, the Little Angels of Korea Folk Ballet, the International Conference on Unified Science, the International Cultural Foundation, Creative Community Project, D.C. Striders Track Club, Collegiate Association for the Research of Principles (CARP), Unification Thought Institute, Council for Unified Research and Education, Sunburst, and New Hope International.

Further moneymaking enterprises include heavy investment in U.S. industry. As early as 1976, the Tonj-II Fishing Company of New York, owned by the Unification Church, bought 5 percent of the entire tuna catch on the Eastern seaboard for export to Japan. The organization owns millions of dollars' worth of fishing and shipping facilities in Massachusetts and Louisiana, as well as armament plants in Korea.

TRANSCENDENTAL MEDITATION

Because Transcendental Meditation combines the attraction of the exotic Eastern way of life with a generous amount of scientific explanation, many Christian and Jewish clergymen have considered it to be non-religious. However, in a famous court suit brought by the Spiritual Counterfeits Project against TM, it was declared that TM teachings are, indeed, religious in nature.

Transcendental Meditation began with Maharashi (Great Seer) Mahesh Yogi (Practicer of Yoga). Born in India in 1918 as Mahesh Prasad Varma, he earned a degree in physics from Allahabad University in 1942 before meeting Swami Brahamanands Saraswati (Guru Dev) and spending thirteen-and-a-half years as his disciple. As the Guru approached death, he charged Maharishi with the responsibility of finding a form of meditation simple enough for everyone to practice. Following two years of solitude in a Himalayan cave, Maharishi introduced TM.

In 1960 Maharishi established the International Meditation Society in London, where he became a hit with the Beatles and a part of a general craze for things Oriental. As the craze faded, and the movement waned among the young and unconventional, it attracted the attention of "straights" who reported that TM made them feel better. Today the movement appears to have greatest strength among young adults, but it has also been well-received by a large number of older persons.

Despite its Hindu influences, TM is a precise set of instructions for leading the meditator into a state of deep rest and heightened signs of relaxation. It demands only twenty minutes of a person's time, morning and evening. This minimal discipline gives one a deep feeling of rest and serenity. Studies at Harvard and several California research centers show the experience to be genuine, health-improving, and the result of autosuggestion.

A course in TM takes the seeker through seven steps: two lectures and an interview with an instructor, followed by four ninety-minute sessions of instruction on meditation, spread over a four-day period.

At the end of a simple initiation ceremony, the student is

assigned a mantra, a word or sound related to Hindu deity that will aid concentration and induce a state of meditation. By silently repeating the mantra, the mind is kept from wandering and the body relaxes as in sleep. The subject is not in a trance, but remains fully awake and able to leave the transcendental state at will, feeling refreshed and rested.

Critics often charge that participation in this ceremony is actual and unknowing worship of the Hindu deity. A portion of the chanting has been translated:

> Offering the invocation to the lotus feet of Shri Guru Dev, I bow down. Offering a seat to the lotus feet of Shri Guru Dev, I bow down. Offering an ablution to the lotus feet of Shri Guru Dev, I bow down. . . . The blinding darkness of ignorance has been removed by applying the balm of knowledge. The eye of knowledge has been opened by him and therefore, to him, to Shri Guru Dev, I bow down.

Of all alternative consciousness movements of recent years, TM has prospered most. In 1975, at its peak growth period, up to fifty-thousand people in the U.S. alone were being initiated into TM each month making an estimated total of one million participants. TM centers have been established in cities across America and in other countries, and Maharishi International University, founded in California in 1972 and now located in Iowa, is dedicated to the integration of all realms of knowledge with the theory and practice of TM.

Part of this rapid spread has been due to cultural conditions in the U.S.—the stress of our rapidly moving society, the economic uncertainties, and emphasis on self-fulfillment.

The true purpose of TM is to alter self and the world to conform to Hinduism's nondualist philosophy—monistic Hinduism. Each TM teacher signs a pledge to the Maharishi which states his recognition of his duty to serve the holy tradition and spread the light of God to all who need it.

THE WAY, INTERNATIONAL (THE WAY BIBLICAL RESEARCH CENTER)

On May 23, 1958, Victor Paul Wierwille resigned the pastorate of St. Peter's Church in Van Wert, Ohio, to found the The Way Biblical Research Center, headquartered on his family farm at New Knoxville, Ohio.

Wierwille, who had studied at Moody Bible Institute, the University of Chicago Divinity School, and Princeton Seminary, was awarded a doctor of theology degree from Pike's Peak Theological Seminary, an alleged degree mill, in 1948.

In 1953, while a minister in the Evangelical and Reformed Church, he began offering a course in "Power for Abundant Living," based upon his private study of Scripture. From 1953 to 1968 his organization made little progress. Then Wierwille became part of California's Jesus Movement, and two years of rapid growth sprouted groups in California, Kansas, North Carolina, and New York.

Wierwille teaches an extreme form of dispensationalism, one premise being that, while all Scripture is inspired, the Old Testament and the Gospels are directed to the Jews and the rest of the New Testament is for Christians. The writings of Paul are particularly important, with the Book of Ephesians holding the highest rank.

Pentecostalism is introduced into the teachings by means of a dozen three-hour tapes which lead the listener into the Charismatic experience, culminating in speaking in tongues. Faith healing is also a part of the cult's teachings.

Wierwille holds a Unitarian, monotheistic position— God is eternal and is in Christ, but because Jesus was born, He is not divine. Instead, Jesus' beginning was conception through God's creation of the soul life in Mary. The soul is equated with life and it is taught that the soul is passed on to children through the sperm of the father.

Wierwille also teaches that Jesus was crucified between four people, two thieves and two malefactors, and he denies baptism on the grounds that water is never mentioned with baptism in the New Testament.

The Way claims not to be a church, yet claims tax exemptions, ordains ministers who perform marriage ceremonies, and is tightly organized into a body modeled after a tree.

The trunk is the international headquarters at New Knoxville; the board of directors is the root; the state organization is the limb; city-wide or regional ministries form branches; local fellowships (in homes or on campuses) are twigs; and individual believers are leaves.

Attenders of "twig meetings" are pressed to enroll in the "Power for Abundant Living" course, at a cost of more than $100. On completion of the course, a member may join Word Over the World or an aggressive evangelism program, The Way Corps.

Genuine commitment begins with enrollment in the Corps, which involves a three-year program conducted at the college campus in Kansas. The program cost more than $300 a month, which must be paid by the member without working during training. Young people are encouraged to write letters of solicitation to acquire this tuition. Life within the Corps is rigidly structured and scheduled, and a time record ("redeemed time analysis") of each day is required. Meals are inadequate and members often become emotionally and physically exhausted. Group control becomes a fact.

Physical culture, including regular daily exercise, is stressed, and a Total Fitness Institute is maintained in California to teach survival skills. In addition, instructions in the use of firearms are included in the curriculum of the center at New Knoxville and at the college in Kansas, supposedly supervised by the Kansas National Guard. No explanation of the need for these types of training has been made.

The Way heavily emphasizes recruitment, as do other cult groups. While the majority of the members are of college age, some older people are also involved. The recruiters make inroads into Fundamentalist and conservative Christian churches and build bridges with these people who share their interest in the Bible. Guilt over the shallowness of one's knowledge of the Scriptures helps convince a prospective member to join the cult.

Large meetings (Rock of Ages Festivals) which feature gospel music are held yearly in New Knoxville and are open to the entire membership, estimated to range between twenty and one hundred thousand. Smaller meetings are also scheduled for members. In 1979 some four thousand Way members went through two weeks of intensive training at Ohio University campus in Athens. Guards surrounded the meetings, refusing entrance to the press or those who had not paid the registration fee of several hundred dollars.

Appendix E—
Addresses of Anticult Organizations

American Family Foundation
  P.O. Box 343
  Lexington, Massachusetts 02173

Citizens Freedom Foundation
  P.O. Box 7000-89
  1719 Via E Prado
  Redondo Beach, California 90277

Committee Engaged in Freeing Minds
  P.O. Box 5084
  Arlington, Texas 76011

COPAC (Citizens Organized for Public Awareness Against
  the Cults)
  P.O. Box 3194
  Greensboro, North Carolina 27402

Citizens Engaged in Reuniting Families
  P.O. Box 348
  Harrison, New York 10052

Ex-members Against Moon
  P.O. Box 62
  Brookline, Massachusetts 02146

Citizens' Freedom Foundation
  P.O. Box 256
  Chula Vista, California 92012

Citizens Engaged in Freeing Minds
P.O. Box 664
Exeter, New Hampshire 02833

Free Minds, Inc.
P.O. Box 4216
Minneapolis, Minnesota 55414

Individual Freedom Foundation
P.O. Box 48
Ardmore, Pennsylvania 19003

Freedom Counseling Center
163 Old Bay Shore Highway, #265
Burlingame, California 94010

Spiritual Counterfeits Project
P.O. Box 4308
Berkeley, California 94704

West Coast Jewish Training Project
190 Denslowe Drive
San Francisco, California 94132

Freeman Cult Prevention
P.O. Box 3598
Akron, Ohio 44310

COMA (Council On Mind Abuse, Inc.)
P.O. Box 575
Station Z
Toronto, Ontario M5N 2Z6
Canada

Appendix F—
A Bill

This bill, introduced in Ohio as House Bill 1037 but subsequently withdrawn, gives an idea of the thinking and goals of anticult legislation.

To amend sections 2111.01, 2111.02, and 2111.04 of the Revised Code to authorize the appointment of temporary guardians in certain situations.

BE IT ENACTED BY THE GENERAL ASSEMBLY OF THE STATE OF OHIO:

Section 1. That sections 2111.01, 2111.02, and 2111.04 of the Revised Code be amended to read as follows:

Sec. 2111.01. As used in Chapters 2101. to 2131. of the Revised Code:

(A) "Guardian," other than a guardian under sections 5905.01 to 5905.19 of the Revised Code, means any person, association, or corporation appointed by the probate court to have the care and management of the person, the estate, or both of an incompetent or minor, or the division of mental retardation and developmental disabilities, an agency under contract with the division for the provision of protective service under sections 5119.85 to 5119.89 of the Revised Code, or the legal rights service created by section 5123.94 of the Revised Code when appointed by the probate court to have the care and management of the person of an incompetent.

(B) "Ward" means any person for whom a guardian as defined in this section is acting.

(C) "Resident guardian" means a guardian appointed by a probate court to have the care and management of property in Ohio belonging to a nonresident ward.

(D) "Incompetent" means any person who by reason of advanced age, improvidence, or mental or physical disability or infirmity, chronic alcoholism, CHRONIC DRUG ABUSE, or mental illness, is incapable of taking proper care of himself or his property or fails to provide for his family or other persons for whom he is charged by law to provide, or any person confined to a penal institution within this state.

"INCAPACITATED" MEANS ANY PERSON WHO IS MENTALLY ABUSED OR EXPLOITED OR IMPROPERLY MANIPULATED SUCH THAT SUFFICIENT EVIDENCE OF AT LEAST TWO OF THE FOLLOWING CONDITIONS EXIST:

(1) PERSONALITY TRAITS OR BEHAVIOR MODES OF THAT PERSON BECOME DRASTICALLY ALTERED, AND MORE OR LESS PERMANENTLY SET, BY ANOTHER OR OTHERS APART FROM THE CONSTRAINTS OF THE FORMAL PRACTICE OF MEDICINE OR PSYCHOLOGY;

(2) THAT PERSON HAVING BEEN INTENTIONALLY OR INADVERTENTLY SUBJECTED TO UNCONSCIONABLE PERSUASION OR TO PROGRESSIVE HYPER-PERSUASIVE PRACTICES OR TO TRANCE INDUCTION PRACTICES OR TO HARSH PSYCHOLOGICAL PRACTICES NOT FORMALLY EMPLOYED SUFFICIENT TO ABRIDGE HIS PERSPECTIVE FOR REALITY TESTING;

(3) THAT PERSON DECEIVED AS TO THE ESSENTIAL NATURE OF SUCH EXPLOITATION SUFFICIENT TO OVERRIDE THE DISCLOSURE OF POSSIBLE HARMS OF HIS PARTICIPATION;

(4) THAT PERSON HAVING BEEN SUBJECTED TO THE EXPOSURE TO AN INDIVIDUAL OR SECT OR OFFSHOOT OF SUCH KNOWN TO EMPLOY AFOREMENTIONED PRACTICES AND/OR DECEPTION;

(5) THAT PERSON BEING INCAPABLE OF MAINTAINING HIS SOCIO-LEGAL REQUIREMENTS;

(6) THAT PERSON WHO IS PHYSICALLY ABUSED OR CONFINED UNDER NON-PENAL REQUIREMENTS, SETTING PERSONALITY TRAITS UPON THAT INDIVIDUAL INCONSISTENT TO HIS PAST GOOD MORALS OR INIMICAL TO THE MORALS OF SOCIETY.

Sec. 2111.02 (A) When found necessary, the probate court on its own motion or an application by any interested party shall appoint a guardian of the person, the estate, or both, of a minor, or incompetent. EXCEPT AS PROVIDED IN DIVISION (F) OF THIS SECTION the person for whom the guardian is to be appointed SHALL BE a resident of the county or HAVE a legal settlement IN THE COUNTY and, except in the case of a minor, SHALL HAVE had the opportunity to have the assistance of counsel in the proceeding for the appointment of such guardian.

(B) AN INTERESTED PARTY WHO APPLIES FOR THE APPOINTMENT OF A GUARDIAN OF THE PERSON, THE ESTATE, OR BOTH, OF AN INCAPACITATED PERSON MAY INCLUDE WITH THE APPLICATION OF INCOMPETENCY AN ALLEGATION THAT FAILURE IMMEDIATELY TO APPOINT A GUARDIAN OF THE PERSON, THE ESTATE, OR BOTH, OF THE INCAPACITATED PERSON WOULD RESULT IN IRREPARABLE

HARM TO THE PERSON, THE ESTATE, OR BOTH, OF THE INCAPACITATED PERSON. THE PROBATE COURT, AFTER A PROCEEDING ON SUCH ALLEGATION, MAY APPOINT A TEMPORARY GUARDIAN OF THE PERSON, THE ESTATE, OR BOTH, OF THE INCAPACITATED PERSON UPON A FINDING THAT FAILURE TO DO SO WOULD RESULT IN IRREPARABLE HARM. A TEMPORARY GUARDIAN APPOINTED UNDER THIS DIVISION HAS ALL OF THE POWERS AND DUTIES OF A GUARDIAN, SUBJECT TO ANY LIMITATIONS IMPOSED BY THE ORDER OF APPOINTMENT, AND SHALL SERVE IN SUCH CAPACITY UNTIL THE PROBATE COURT HOLDS A FULL HEARING ON THE APPLICATION FOR THE APPOINTMENT OF A GUARDIAN OF THE PERSON OR ESTATE OR BOTH, IN ACCORDANCE WITH SECTION 2111.04 OF THE REVISED CODE, OR SUCH SHORTER PERIOD OF TIME AS THE COURT DIRECTS IN THE ORDER OF APPOINTMENT.

(C) If a person is incompetent due to physical disability the consent of the incompetent must first be obtained before the appointment of a guardian for him, and such person may select a guardian who shall be appointed if a suitable person.

(D) The guardian of an incompetent, by virtue of such appointment shall be the guardian of the minor children of his ward, unless the court appoints some other person as their guardian.

(E) When the primary purpose of the appointment of a guardian is, or was, the collection, disbursement, or administration of moneys awarded by the veterans administration to the ward, or assets derived thereof, no court costs shall be charged in the proceeding for the appointment or in any subsequent proceedings made in pursuance of the appointment, unless the value of the estate, including the moneys then due under the veterans administration award, exceeds one thousand five hundred dollars.

(F) THE PERSON FOR WHOM THE GUARDIAN IS TO BE APPOINTED NEED NOT BE A RESIDENT OF THE COUNTY OR HAVE A LEGAL SETTLEMENT IN THE COUNTY IN ORDER FOR THE PROBATE COURT TO APPOINT A GUARDIAN OF THE PERSON, HIS ESTATE, OR BOTH, WHEN ALL OF THE FOLLOWING APPLY:

(1) THE PERSON DOES NOT RESIDE OR HAVE A LEGAL SETTLEMENT IN THIS STATE;

(2) AN INTERESTED PARTY, WHO IS A RESIDENT OF THE COUNTY OR HAS A LEGAL SETTLEMENT IN THE COUNTY, AND IS A RELATIVE OF THE PERSON, FILES AN APPLICATION FOR THE APPOINTMENT OF THE GUARDIAN;

(3) THE PERSON IS INCAPACITATED.

Sec. 2111.04 (A) No guardian of the person, the estate, or both OTHER THAN A TEMPORARY GUARDIAN AS APPOINTED UNDER SECTION 2111.02 OF THE REVISED CODE FOR AN INCAPACITATED PERSON shall be appointed until at least three days after the probate court has caused written notice, setting forth the time and place of the FULL hearing, to be served upon the following persons:

(1) In the appointment of the guardian of a minor, notice shall be served:

    (*a*) Upon the minor, if over the age of fourteen years, by personal service;

    (*b*) Upon each parent of the minor whose name and address are known or can with reasonable diligence be ascertained, provided the parent is free from disability other than minority;

    (*c*) Upon the next of kin of the minor known to reside in the county in which application is made, if there is no living parent, the name and address of the parent cannot be ascertained, or the parent is under disability other than minority;

    (*d*) Upon the person having the custody of the minor.

(2) In the appointment of the guardian of an incompetent, notice shall be served;

    (*a*) Upon the person for whom appointment is sought by personal service OR, IF THE PERSON FOR WHOM APPOINTMENT IS SOUGHT DOES NOT RESIDE IN OR HAVE LEGAL SETTLEMENT IN THIS STATE, BY CERTIFIED MAIL SERVICE OR PERSONAL SERVICE;

    (*b*) Upon the next of kin of the person for whom appointment is sought known to reside in the county in which application is made.

    Notice may not be waived by the person for whom the appointment is sought.

    From the service of notice until the hearing, no sale, gift, conveyance, or encumbrance of the property of the incompetent shall be valid as to all persons having notice of the proceeding.

(B) (1) UPON APPLICATION FOR THE APPOINTMENT OF A TEMPORARY GUARDIAN OF THE PERSON, THE ESTATE, OR BOTH, OF AN INCAPACITATED PERSON AS DESCRIBED IN DIVISION (B) OF SECTION 2111.02 OF THE REVISED CODE, THE PROBATE

Dealing With Destructive Cults

COURT SHALL CAUSE SUCH NOTICE AS IT DETERMINES FEASIBLE UNDER THE CIRCUMSTANCES TO BE SERVED UNDER THIS SECTION, NONETHELESS FULFILLING THE NOTICE REQUIREMENTS PRIOR TO THE FULL HEARING. THE PROBATE COURT SHALL CONDUCT A HEARING ON THE ALLEGATIONS CONTAINED IN THE APPLICATION, WHICH HEARING MAY BE HELD EX PARTE IF THE COURT DETERMINES THE ALLEGATIONS REQUIRE SUCH URGENCY.

(2) THE COURT SHALL HOLD A FULL HEARING FOR INCOMPETENCY BY THE END OF THIRTY DAYS IN THE CASE OF AN INCAPACITATED PERSON UNLESS ONE OF THE FOLLOWING CONDITIONS EXIST:

(a) THE WARD REQUESTS A CONTINUANCE OF SAID TEMPORARY GUARDIANSHIP FOR A NON-RENEWABLE EXTENSION OF THIRTY ADDITIONAL DAYS;

(b) THE TEMPORARY GUARDIAN PETITIONS THE COURT FOR HIS RESIGNATION AND FOR THE ABANDONMENT AND RECISION OF THE APPLICATION;

(c) THE TEMPORARY GUARDIAN PETITIONS FOR A NON-RENEWABLE EXTENSION OF SAID TEMPORARY GUARDIANSHIP FOR THIRTY ADDITIONAL DAYS.

Section 2. That existing sections 2111.01, 2111.02, and 2111.04 of the Revised Code are hereby repealed.

Bibliography

The following bibliography lists general works on cults and related subjects. Out-of-print publications may be available in libraries.

Anderson, J. N. D. *The World's Religions.* Grand Rapids: William B. Eerdmans Publishing Co. 1976. (out of print)

Bach, Marcus. *Major Religions of the World.* New York: Abingdon Press, 1959.

———*Strangers at the Door.* Nashville: Abingdon Press, 1971. (out of print)

Barreau, Jean-Claude. *The Religious Impulse.* New York: Paulist Press, 1979.

Berger, Peter. *The Sacred Canopy.* New York: Doubleday and Co., Inc., 1967.

Berry, Harold J. *Examining the Cults.* Lincoln, Nebr.: Back to the Bible, 1977. (pamphlet)

———*Witnessing to the Cults.* Lincoln, Nebr.: Back to the Bible, 1974. (pamphlet)

Bjornstad, James. *Counterfeits at Your Door.* Glendale, Calif.: Regal Books, 1979.

Boa, Kenneth. *Cults, World Religions, and You.* Wheaton, Ill.: Victor Books, 1977.

Breese, Dave. *Know the Marks of Cults.* Wheaton, Ill.: Victor Books, 1975.

———*The Marks of a Cult.* Lincoln, Nebr.: Back to the Bible, 1973. (pamphlet)

Bromley, David G. and Shupe, Anson D., Jr. *Strange Gods: The Great American Cult Scare.* Boston: Beacon Press, 1981.

Burstein, Abraham. *Religion, Cults, and the Law.* Dobbs Ferry, N.Y.: Oceana Publications, 1980.

Caplovitz, David and Sherrow, Fred. *The Religious Drop-outs.* Beverly Hills, Calif.: SAGE Publications, 1977.

Cinnamon, Kenneth and Farson, Dave. *Cults and Cons*. Chicago: Nelson-Hall, Inc., 1979.

Clark, Elmer T. *The Small Sects in America*. Magnolia, Mass.: Peter Smith Publisher, Inc.

Clark, John. *Testimony to Vermont Senate on Cults*. Pittsburgh: P.A.I.F. (pamphlet)

Clements, R. D. *God and the Gurus*. Downers Grove, Ill.: Inter-Varsity Press, 1975.

Cohen, Daniel. *The New Believers*. New York: M. Evans and Co., Inc., 1975.

Connor, Robert. *Walled In*. New York: The New American Library, Inc., 1979. (out of print)

Conway, Flo and Siegelman, Jim. *Snapping: America's Epidemic of Sudden Personality Change*. Philadelphia: J. B. Lippincott Co., 1978. (out of print)

Davies, Horton. *The Challenge of the Sects*. Philadelphia: The West-minster Press, 1961. (out of print)

Edwards, Christopher. *Crazy for God*. Englewood Cliffs, N.J.: Prentice-Hall, Inc., 1979.

Elkins, Chris. *Heavenly Deception*. Wheaton, Ill.: Tyndale House Publishers, Inc., 1980.

Ellul, Jacques. *Propaganda*. New York: Vintage Books, 1973.

Ellwood, Robert S. *Alternative Altars: Unconventional and Eastern Spirituality in America*. Chicago: University of Chicago Press, 1981.

———*Many Peoples, Many Faiths*. Englewood Cliffs, N.J.: Prentice-Hall, Inc., 1973.

Enroth, Ronald M. *The Lure of the Cults*. Chappaqua, N.Y.: Christian Herald Books, 1979.

———*Youth, Brainwashing, and the Extremist Cults*. Grand Rapids: Zondervan Publishing House, 1977.

Frank, Jerome D. *Persuasion and Healing*. New York: Schocken Books, 1961.

Fromm, Erich. *Escape from Freedom*. New York: Avon Books, 1965.

Galper, Mertin. *Report on Cultic Brainwash*. Redondo Beach, Calif.: Freedom Foundation. (pamphlet)

Glock, Charles Y. and Bellah, Robert N., eds. *The New Religious Consciousness*. Los Angeles: University of California Press, 1976.

Grant, J. *The Enemy*. Wheaton, Ill.: Tyndale House Publishers, Inc., 1973.

Greenfield, Robert. *Spiritual Supermarket.* New York: Saturday Review Press, 1975.

Guinness, Os. *The East: No Exit.* Downers Grove, Ill.: Inter-Varsity Press, 1974. (out of print)

Heenan, Edward. *Mystery, Magic, and Miracle.* Englewood Cliffs, N.J.: Prentice-Hall, Inc., 1973.

Hefley, James C. *The Youth Nappers.* Wheaton, Ill.: Victor Books, 1977.

Hoekema, Anthony A. *The Four Major Cults.* Grand Rapids: William B. Eerdmans Publishing Co., 1963.

Hoffer, E. *The True Believer.* New York: Harper & Row, Publishers, Inc., 1951.

Hultquist, Lee. *They Followed the Piper.* Plainfield, N.J.: Logos International, 1977.

Lanternari, Vittorio. *The Religions of the Oppressed.* New York: Mentor Books, 1969. (out of print)

Lifton, Robert J. *Thought Reform and the Psychology of Totalism.* New York: W. W. Norton and Co., Inc., 1961.

Lohmeyer, Ernst. *Lord of the Temple: A Study of the Relation Between Cult and Gospel.* Geneva, Ala.: Allenson-Brekenridge, 1961.

McBeth, L. *Strange New Religions.* Nashville: Broadman Press, 1977.

McConahy, John G. *Address to Seminar, LaRoche College, 1977— General Commentary on Cult Techniques and Physiological Causes.* Pittsburgh: P.A.I.F. (pamphlet)

MacCollan, Joel A. *Carnival of Souls.* New York: The Seabury Press, 1979. (out of print)

Martin, M. *Hostage to the Devil.* New York: Bantam Books, 1976.

Martin, Rachel and Young, Bonnie P. *Escape.* Denver: Accent Books, 1979.

Martin, Walter R. *The Kingdom of the Cults.* Minneapolis: Bethany House, 1968.

_____*The New Cults.* Santa Ana, Calif.: Vision House, 1980.

_____*Rise of the Cults.* Santa Ana, Calif.: Vision House, 1980.

Marty, Martin E. *A Nation of Behavers.* Chicago: The University of Chicago Press, 1976.

_____*The Pro and Con Book of Religious America.* Waco, Texas: Word Books, 1975.

Maslow, Abraham H. *Toward a Psychology of Being.* New York: Van Nostrand, 1968.

Mayer, F. E. *The Religious Bodies of America*. St. Louis: Concordia Publishing House, 1956. (out of print)

Means, Pat. *The Mystical Maze*. San Bernardino, Calif.: Campus Crusade for Christ, 1976.

Meerloo, Joost, A. M. *Rape of the Mind*. New York: Grosset & Dunlap, 1961.

Melton, J. Gordon. *Encyclopedia of American Religions*. Wilmington, N.C.: McGrath Publishing Co., 1978.

Merrit, Jean. *Comments on Cults*. Pittsburgh: P.A.I.F. (pamphlet)

——*Coping with Cults*. Pittsburgh: P.A.I.F. (pamphlet)

Milgram, Stanley. *Obedience to Authority*. New York: Harper & Row, Publishers, Inc., 1974.

Moody, Jess. *The Jesus Freaks*. Waco, Tex.: Word Books, 1971. (out of print)

Moore, E. Garth. *Try the Spirits*. New York: Oxford University Press, 1977.

Morgan, Richard E. *The Politics of Religious Conflict*. New York: Pegasus, 1968.

Needleman, Jacob. *The New Religions*. New York: E. P. Dutton, 1977.

—— and Baker, George, eds. *Understanding the New Religions*. New York: Seabury Press, 1978. (out of print)

Noss, John B. *Man's Religions*. New York: Macmillan Publishing Co., Inc., 1980.

Niebuhr, H. Richard. *The Social Sources of Denominationalism*. Magnolia, Mass.: Peter Smith Publisher, Inc.

Patrick, Ted. *Let Our Children Go!* New York: Ballantine Books, 1976. (out of print)

Peterson, William J. *Those Curious New Cults*. New Canaan, Conn.: Keats Publishing, 1976.

Rader, Stanley R. *Against the Gates of Hell*. New York: Everest House Publishers, 1980.

Rexroth, Kenneth. *Communalism: From Its Origins to the Twentieth Century*. New York: The Seabury Press, 1974. (out of print)

Richardson, J. T., ed. *Conversion Careers: In and Out of the New Religions*. Beverly Hills, Calif.: SAGE Publications, 1978.

Ridenour, Fritz. *So What's the Difference?* Ventura, Calif.: Regal Books, 1979.

Robbins, Thomas, and Anthony, Dick, eds. *In Gods We Trust: New Patterns of Religious Pluralism in America*. New Brunswick, N.J.: Transaction Books, 1981.

Robertson, Irvine. *What the Cults Believe*, 2nd. Ed. Chicago: Moody Press, 1979.

Rodgers, William D. *Cult Sunday*. Denver: Accent Books, 1979.

Rose, Stephen. *Jesus and Jim Jones*. New York: Pilgrim Press, 1979.

Rudin, A. James and Marcia R. *Prison or Paradise? The New Religious Cults*. Philadelphia: Fortress Press, 1980.

Sargent, William. *The Mind Possessed*. New York: Penguin Books, 1975.

Shupe, Anson D., Jr., and Bromley, David G. *A Documentary History of the American Anti-cult Movement*. New York: The Edwin Mellen Press, 1981.

_____*A Role Theory Approach to Participation in Religious Movements*. Arlington: University of Texas, 1978.

_____*The New Vigilantes: Deprogrammers, Anti-cultists, and the New Religions*. Beverly Hills, Calif.: SAGE Publications, 1980.

_____*Six Alternative Perspectives on New Religions: A Case Study Approach*. New York: The Edwin Mellen Press, 1981.

Soblien, Paul D. *Mind Control Techniques by Pseudo-religious Cults*. Bird Island, Minn.: Our Savior's Lutheran Church. (pamphlet)

Sparks, Jack. *The Mindbenders: A Look at Current Cults*. New York: Thomas Nelson, Inc., 1977.

Spittler, Russell P. *Cults and Isms*. Grand Rapids: Baker Book House, 1973.

Stoner, Carroll and Parke, Jo Anne. *All God's Children: The Cult Experience*. Radnor Pa.: Chilton Book Co., 1977.

Streiker, Lowell D. *The Cults Are Coming*. Nashville: Abingdon Press, 1978.

Thielicke, Helmut. *Between God and Satan*. Grand Rapids: Zondervan Publishing House, 1958.

Thielmann, Bonnie. *The Broken God*. Elgin, Ill.: David C. Cook Publishers, 1979.

Ungerleider, J. Thomas. *The New Religions: Insights into the Cult Phenomenon*. New York: Merck, Sharp and Dohme, 1979.

Verdier, Paul A. *Brainwashing and the Cults: An Expose on Capturing the Human Mind*. Los Angeles: Wilshire Publishers, 1977.

Watson, Tex. *Will You Die for Me?* Old Tappan, N.J.: Fleming H. Revell Co., 1978. (out of print)

Whalen, William J. *Minority Religions in America*. Staten Island, N.Y.: Alba House, 1981.

White, Mel. *Deceived*. Old Tappan, N.J.: Spire Books, 1979.

Wilburn, Gary A. *The Fortune Sellers,* Glendale, Calif.. Gospel Light Publications, 1972. (out of print)

Wuthnow, Robert. *Experimentation in American Religion: The New Mysticisms and Their Implications for the Churches.* Berkeley: University of California Press, 1978.

Yanoff, Morris. *Where is Joey?* Athens: Ohio University Press, 1982.

Zaretsky, Irving and Leone, Mark. *Religious Movements in Contemporary America.* Princeton, N.J.: Princeton University Press, 1974.

The following bibliography lists works on specific cults. Out-of-print publications may be available in libraries.

The Children of God

Hopkins, Joseph. "Children of God: Disciples of Deception." *Christianity Today* reprint #19, c 1977.

Lefkowitz, Lewis. "Final Report on Children of God." Charity Frauds Bureau, World Trade Bldg., New York, N.Y.

McManus, Una and Cooper, John Charles. *Not for a Million Dollars.* Nashville: Impact Books, 1980.

The Divine Light Mission

Downton, James V. Jr. *Sacred Journey: Conversion and Commitment to Divine Light Mission.* New York: Columbia University Press, 1979.

Hare Krishna (ISKCON)

Levine, Faye. *The Strange World of the Hare Krishnas.* New York: Fawcett, 1974.

Yamamoto, J. Isamu. *Hare Krishna, Hare Krishna.* Downers Grove, Ill.: Inter-Varsity Press, 1978.

Transcendental Meditation

Carlson, Ronald L. *Transcendental Meditation: Relation or Religion?* Chicago: Moody Press, 1978.

Haddon David, *Transcendental Meditation.* Downers Grove, Ill.: Inter-Varsity Press, 1975.

Johnson, William A. *The Search for Transcendence.* New York: Harper & Row, Publishers, Inc., 1974.

Unification Church

Bjornstad, James. *The Moon Is Not the Son.* Minneapolis: Bethany House, 1977.

Bromley, David G. and Shupe, Anson D., Jr. *Moonies in America: Cults, Church, and Crusade.* Beverly Hills, Calif.: SAGE Publications, 1979.

Horowitz, Irving Louis, ed. *Science Sin and Scholarship: The Politics of Reverend Moon and the Unification Church.* Cambridge, Mass.: MIT Press, 1978.

Levitt, Zola. *The Spirit of Sun Myung Moon.* Irvine, Calif.: Harvest House Publishers, 1976. (out of print)

Sontag, Frederick. *Sun Myung Moon and the Unification Church.* Nashville: Abingdon Press, 1977. (out of print)

Wood, Allen Tate with Vitek, Jack. *Moonstruck: A Memoir of My Life in a Cult.* New York: William Morrow & Co., Inc., 1979.

Yamamoto, J. Isamu. *The Moon Doctrine.* Downers Grove, Ill.: Inter-Varsity Press, 1976.

The Way, International

MacCollam, Joe A. *The Way of Victor Paul Wierwille.* Downers Grove, Ill.: Inter-Varsity Press, 1978.

Williams, J. L. *Victor Paul Wierwille and the Way International.* Chicago: Moody Press, 1979.

Various tapes on specific cults are available from:

One Way Library	Walk Through the Bible
Division of Vision House Publishers	Ministries
1651 E. Edinger	603 West Peachtree St., NE
Suite 104	Atlanta, Georgia 30308
Santa Ana, California 92705	

The following bibliography lists publications produced by the various cultic groups. They are not recommended for reading, other than for research purposes.

Children of God

Hebron, Jeremiah. *Psalm 23.* Rome: Children of God, 1977.

Pictorial Scripture Book. Rome: Children of God, 1978.

Following are some of the titles of the "MO Letters":

"Flirty Fishing"	"I Am a Toilet"

"Ask Any Communist"
"Bewitched"
"Brother Sun"
"The Crazy Crusade"
"Child Brides"
"Homos"
"Drop Outs"
"Revolutionary Sex"
"He Stands in the Gap"

"Jesus People Revolution"
"Mountin' Maid"
"Paper Agape"
"Rasputin, Hero or Hell?"
"Sex Works"
"Women in Love"
"There Are No Neutrals"
"Who Are the Rebels?"

Eckankar

Twitchell, Paul. *Eckankar: The Key to Secret Worlds.* San Diego: Illuminated Way Press, 1969.

Hare Krishna (ISKCON)

Prabhapada, A. C. Bhaktivedanta Swami. *Beyond Birth and Death.* Los Angeles: Bhaktivedanta Book Trust.

——*Bhagavad-gita, As it is.* Los Angeles: Bhaktivedanta Book Trust.

——*Dialectical Spiritualism—A Vedic View of Western Philosophy.* Los Angeles: Bhaktivedanta Book Trust.

——*Easy Journey to Other Planets.* Los Angeles: Bhaktivedanta Book Trust.

——*Elevation to Krsna Consciousness.* Los Angeles: Bhaktivedanta Book Trust.

——*Geetar-gan* (Bengali). Los Angeles: Bhaktivedanta Book Trust.

——*Krsna Consciousness: The Matchless Gift.* Los Angeles: Bhaktivedanta Book Trust.

——*Krsna Consciousness: The Topmost Yoga System.* Los Angeles: Bhaktivedanta Book Trust.

——*Krsna, the Reservoir of Pleasure.* Los Angeles: Bhaktivedanta Book Trust.

——*Krsna, the Supreme Personality of Godhead,* 3 vols. Los Angeles: Bhaktivedanta Book Trust.

——*Life Comes From Life.* Los Angeles: Bhaktivedanta Book Trust.

——*The Nectar of Devotion.* Los Angeles: Bhaktivedanta Book Trust.

——*The Nectar of Instruction.* Los Angeles: Bhaktivedanta Book Trust.

——*On the Way to Krsna.* Los Angeles: Bhaktivedanta Book Trust.

——*Perfect Questions, Perfect Answers.* Los Angeles: Bhaktivedanta Book Trust.

_____*The Perfection of Yoga*. Los Angeles: Bhaktivedanta Book Trust.

_____*Raja-vidya: The King of Knowledge*. Los Angeles: Bhaktivedanta Book Trust.

_____*Sri Caitanya-caritamtra*, 17 vols. Los Angeles: Bhaktivedanta Book Trust.

_____*Sri Isopanisad*. Los Angeles: Bhaktivedanta Book Trust.

_____*Srimad-Bahagavatam, Cantos 1–10*, 50 vols. Los Angeles: Bhaktivedanta Book Trust.

_____*Teachings of Lord Caitanya*. Los Angeles: Bhaktivedanta Book Trust.

_____*Teaching of Lord Kapila, the Son of Devhuti*. Los Angeles: Bhaktivedanta Book Trust.

_____*Transcendental Teachings of Prahlad Maharaja*. Los Angeles: Bhaktivedanta Book Trust.

The magazine *Back to Godhead* is also published by the ISKCON organization.

Unification Church

Bryant, David and Hodges, Susan, eds. *Exploring Unification Theology*. Barrytown, N.Y.: The Rose of Sharon Press, Inc., 1978.

Bryant, David and Foster, Durwood, eds. *Hermeneutics and Unification Theology*. Barrytown, N.Y.: The Rose of Sharon Press, Inc., 1980.

Bryant, David., ed. *Proceedings of the Virgin Islands' Seminar on Unification Theology*. Barrytown, N.Y.: The Rose of Sharon Press, Inc., 1979.

Lewis, Warren, ed. *Towards a Global Congress of the World's Religions*. Barrytown, N.Y.: Unification Theological Seminary, vol. 1, 1978; vol. 2, 1979; vol. 3, 1980.

Truth Is My Sword. New York: Unification Church of America, 1978.

Unification Thought. New York: Unification Thought Institute, 1973.

The Way, International

Cummins, Walter J. *Fruit of the Spirit*. New Knoxville, Ohio: American Christian Press.

_____*The Gifts of God*. New Knoxville, Ohio: American Christian Press.

_____*The Mind of the Believer*. New Knoxville, Ohio: American Christian Press.

Johnson, Lonnell E. *The Gift.* New Knoxville, Ohio: American Christian Press.

Owens, Dorothy. *Christian Etiquette.* New Knoxville, Ohio: American Christian Press.

——*Keys to Spiritual Light.* New Knoxville, Ohio: American Christian Press.

Wade, Peter J. *I Can Do All Things.* New Knoxville, Ohio: American Christian Press.

——*Receiving Your Answer from God.* New Knoxville, Ohio: American Christian Press.

——*The Secret of Radiant Living.* New Knoxville, Ohio: American Christian Press.

Wierwille, Victor Paul. *Are the Dead Alive Now?* Old Greenwich, Conn.: Delvin-Adair, 1971.

——*The Bible Tells Me So.* New Knoxville, Ohio: American Christian Press.

——*Christians Should Be Prosperous.* New Knoxville, Ohio: American Christian Press.

——*The Church (The Great Mystery Revealed).* New Knoxville, Ohio: American Christian Press.

——*God's Magnified Word.* New Knoxville, Ohio: American Christian Press, 1977.

——*Jesus Christ Is Not God.* New Knoxville, Ohio: American Christian Press, 1975.

——*The New, Dynamic Church.* New Knoxville, Ohio: American Christian Press, 1971.

——*Power for Abundant Living.* New Knoxville, Ohio: American Christian Press, 1971.

——*Receiving the Holy Spirit Today.* New Knoxville, Ohio: American Christian Press, 1972.

——*Studies in Human Suffering.* New Knoxville, Ohio: American Christian Press.

——*The Word Way.* New Knoxville, Ohio: American Christian Press, 1971.

Wyan, Rachel. *Kept By God's Power.* New Knoxville, Ohio: American Christian Press.

The "Power for Abundant Living" Course includes these volumes:
Foundational Class-Power for Abundant Living. New Knoxville, Ohio: American Christian Press.

Home Study Lessons. New Knoxville, Ohio: American Christian Press.

These periodicals are published by the Way, International:

Heart. (bimonthly)

The Way. (semimonthly)